THE
GOOD COMPANIONS

A Play in Two Acts

BY
J. B. PRIESTLEY
AND
EDWARD KNOBLOCK
(From the Novel by J. B. PRIESTLEY)

SAMUEL FRENCH LIMITED
LONDON

FOR AMATEUR PRODUCTION ENQUIRIES

UNITED KINGDOM AND WORLD EXCLUDING NORTH AMERICA
plays@SamuelFrench-London.co.uk
020 7255 4302/01

Each title is subject to availability from Samuel French, depending upon country of performance.

THE GOOD COMPANIONS

Produced at His Majesty's Theatre, Haymarket, London, on May 14th, 1931, with the following cast of characters :

MRS. OAKROYD	Beatrix Feilden-Kaye.
SAM OGLETHORPE	Frank Pettingell.
JESS OAKROYD	Edward Chapman.
LEONARD OAKROYD	Clive Morton.
ALBERT TUGGERIDGE	Jack Clewes.
ELIZABETH TRANT	Edith Sharpe.
LANDLORD AT TUMBLEBY	William Heilbronn.
EFFIE (Barmaid)	Ellen Pollock.
INIGO JOLLIFANT	John Gielgud.
MR. FAUNTLEY	Deering Wells.
SUSIE DEAN	Adele Dixon.
MORTON MITCHAM	Lawrence Baskcomb.
MRS. TARVIN	Constance Anderson.
MR. TARVIN	Mark Turner.
JOBY JACKSON	Alexander Field.
PROFESSOR MIRO	Max Montesole.
LINOLEUM MAN	William Heilbronn.
ENVELOPE MAN	Larry O'Brien.
SUMMERS	James Stadden.
POLICEMAN AT RIBSDEN	Nat Lewis.
JIMMY NUNN	Edwin Ellis.
ELSIE LONGSTAFF	Ellen Pollock.
JOE BRUNDIT	Bernard Dudley.
MRS. JOE BRUNDIT	Viola Compton.
MRS. MAUNDERS	Margaret Yarde.
JERRY JERNINGHAM	Jack Clewes.
LADY PARTLIT	Margaret Yarde.
MR. DULVER	Gerald Hornby.
WAITER (at the " Royal Standard," Rawsley)	Clive Morton.
PHOTOGRAPHER (at Gatford)	Max Montesole.
REPORTER	Deering Wells.
LANDLORD (of the " Crown," Gatford)	Mark Turner.
RIDVERS	William Heilbronn.
MR. PITSNER	Alexander Field.
ETHEL GEORGIA	Dorothy Seacombe.
MONTE MORTIMER	Nat Lewis.
MR. GOOCH	Deering Wells.

Market people at Ribsden. Guests at Gatford.
Audience and roughs at Gatford.

The Play produced by JULIAN WYLIE.

SCENES

ACT I

ACT II

(Six months later)

THE GOOD COMPANIONS

ACT I

Scene 1

Scene.—*Living-room at Oakroyd's house, Bruddersford.*

Time.—*It is early evening in autumn.*

Back R.C. *door to street.* L.C. *window to street. In* L. *wall,* C. *fireplace with a great many clothes in front of it on a clothes-horse.* R. *wall, up stage, door to scullery; down stage, door to upstairs. In the* C. *of the room is a table, part of which is occupied by tea-things and the rest by clothes, iron, etc.*

(See Photograph of Scene. Small set.)

As Curtain *rises,* Mrs. Oakroyd, *a hard woman of forty-five, is discovered behind clothes-horse with left hand on kettle and poking to make kettle boil. She lifts kettle back on to hob* L. *of fireplace, and places poker in corner* R. *of fireplace, and comes out from behind clothes-horse. She then wipes her hands on her apron, picks shirt off horse and crosses to table* C. *as* Leonard *shakes spoon. She shakes out the shirt, puts it on table and goes on with dialogue.*

Oglethorpe, *a stout, good-natured man of fifty, neat and respectable, is seated at the table* R. *Also* Leonard, *twenty-one,* L.

As Curtain *rises* Leonard *pours himself out a cup of tea, takes spoon out of sugar-basin, stirs his tea with it, shakes the moisture off and wipes it on tablecloth, and replaces it in sugar-basin.*

Mrs. Oakroyd (*behind table* C.). Have you got all you want, love ?
Leonard (L.). Yes, I think so, mother.
Mrs. Oakroyd. Nay, you haven't. I've a nice bit o' pasty in there for you. You'd like that, wouldn't you, love ?

(Goes out up R., *taking plate with kipper bone from table.)*

Leonard. I expect you've had your tea, haven't you, Mr. Oglethorpe ?
Oglethorpe. Aye, long since. I've been up to t' Quack Market and sold a few pullets. They tak' too much rearing up yonder. I thowt I'd look in to see your father. He's late.

*(*Mrs. Oakroyd *returns from up* R. *with pasty and comes to* C.)*

MRS. OAKROYD. Late! I should think he *is* late. I've had his tea ready nearly an hour and a half. Can't think what's keeping him. Some piece o' silliness, I'll be bound. Here's your pasty, love. (*Places pasty on table before* LEONARD.)

OGLETHORPE. 'Ar's your Jess going on, Mrs. Oakroyd? Is he wanting to go on his travels ageean—down south, eh?

MRS. OAKROYD (*arranging shirt on table*). He's like t' rest o' you men. He's pinin' for summat, but he doesn't knaw what. (*Holds iron to cheek.*) An' don't you go puttin' onny wrong ideas in his head. (*Points at* OGLETHORPE *with iron and crosses to fireplace to change iron.*)

OGLETHORPE. Me? Na, nay. You don't catch me puttin' onny ideas o' onny kind in onnybody's head.

(MRS. OAKROYD *returns to table and goes on ironing.*)

MRS. OAKROYD. I'll tell you this much. . . . If it wasn't for our Leonard here, I don't know where I'd be. Makking more money nor his father now.

OGLETHORPE. Aye, shavin' t' nobs, aren't yer now, lad?

LEONARD. That's right. Just started at Gregson's.

MRS. OAKROYD. And how much did you mak' in tips to-day, love?

LEONARD. Eight and threepence.

MRS. OAKROYD. There you are. What d'you think o' that, Mr. Oglethorpe? His father'll have to tak' back seat after this. (*Puts iron down and moves* L.C. *of table.*)

OGLETHORPE. Aye, maybe.

(*Enter* ALBERT TUGGERIDGE, *a silly youth of twenty, up* R.C., *with a dilapidated suitcase and box under his arm.*)

ALBERT (C.). Hello, hello, hello, there! Here we are! The old firm. Good evening, Mrs. Oakroyd. I've come.

(LEONARD *rises and goes up* L.C.)

MRS. OAKROYD (L.C.). My word, you have an' all.

ALBERT (C.). I've brought all my stuff round but the gramophone. Do you think it'll be all reight?

LEONARD (L.C.). Of course it'll be all reight. Won't it, mother?

ALBERT. Does your *father* know I'm coming? Have you told him?

MRS. OAKROYD. He doesn't know yet. He's not back from his work. He's late. This is summat he's going to learn.

LEONARD (L.C.). Put your things down there, Albert. (*Pointing to corner under gas* L.)

ALBERT. You're sure it'll be all reight? You see, I thought it was settled. (*Crosses and puts bags down in corner* L.)

MRS. OAKROYD (*comes down to table,* L.C.). Well, if it isn't now it soon will be. If he tries to make a fuss, I'll tell him straight.

You're our Leonard's friend, and he wants you here. And so do
I. We've room. Ever since our Lily got married and went off
to Canada, that room up there's been empty and doing nowt—just
because his lordship won't have onnybody else in the house. Well,
he'll have to think different now—that's all—or t' fat 'ull be in t'
fire. (*Goes back to shirt on table* c.)

ALBERT (*down* L.). Not so nice, though, when the fat is in t' fire.
It burnt me a bit, last time.

OGLETHORPE. An' 'ar's your Lily and her husband goin' i'
Canada ?

MRS. OAKROYD (c.). Oh, you mun ask her father about our Lily.
She writes to him, not to me. (*Folds shirt up and puts it down on* R.
of table by the iron.)

ALBERT. Look here, I'll just pop back. (*Crosses* LEONARD *to*
L.C.) I've got to get the gramophone, anyhow—and no doubt
you'll have settled it before I get back.

MRS. OAKROYD (*listening, then going up to window* L.C.). He's
coming. I know his step.

ALBERT (*crossing* MRS. OAKROYD *and going to door* R.C.). Here,
I'm off. I can just slip down the other way. Toodle-oo.

(*He hurries out off* R.C., *followed by* LEONARD.)

MRS. OAKROYD (*picking up teapot and crossing to the fireplace*).
Well, he won't be any too pleased with his kipper. It's been
shrivelling up steady for t' last hour. (*Fills pot from kettle.*)

(*Enter* JESS OAKROYD, *door* R.C., *from street* L., *carrying a bag of
tools. He is a stocky, shrewd, kindly man of forty-seven. He
leaves the door open.*)

OGLETHORPE. Na, Jess lad.

OAKROYD (*going to sofa* L.C.). Na, Sam. (*He flings down his bag
of tools on the sofa* L.C.)

OGLETHORPE. And where have you been till this time ?

OAKROYD (L.C.). Been on to t' Union Office.

(LEONARD *returns, smoking cigarette. He closes the door and stands
by it* R.C.)

MRS. OAKROYD. Whatever for ?

OAKROYD. 'Cos I've been stopped.

(LEONARD *stops. Suddenly looks at* OAKROYD.)

MRS. OAKROYD (L.). You've been what ?

OAKROYD (L.C.). Stopped, sacked, paid off, kicked aht, whativver
you want to call it. (*Throws down Insurance card and some money
on the table.*) Higden's has finished wi' me, and me wi' them. (*Puts
cap on sofa.*) There's a week's money there. Mak' most of it.
My tea ready ? (*Sits behind table,* c.)

MRS. OAKROYD (L.C., *giving him his tea in teapot and placing kipper
on table*). But what 'a' you been doing ? (*Stands* L. *of table.*)

OGLETHORPE. Nay, Jess lad.

OAKROYD. Aye, Sam, it's a poor do. Hello, what's this?
(*Examines kipper.*) By gow, you've given this a bit o' fire, haven't
you? It's nobbut like a lead pencil. (*Pushes plate away.*)

MRS. OAKROYD. Happen it's t' last you'll see for a bit, at any
rate. What you gotten stopped for?

OAKROYD. For nowt. Nowt at all. For being a man and not
a damned monkey. (*Pours himself out a cup of tea.*) This morning
I hadn't a waggon in and were doing nowt for a bit, so Simpson,
t' under manager—you knaw, Sam——

OGLETHORPE. Aye, lad, I do.

OAKROYD. He says, "Here, Oakroyd, you're doing nowt. Give
'em a hand with that gutter on that temporary shed over yon."
(*Puts teapot down, picks up milk.*) So I takes a length o' gutter and
starts fixing it up.

OGLETHORPE. Same as onnybody might 'a' done.

OAKROYD. Aye, but owd on a bit. A feller comes up, one o'
t' shop steward, d'you see. He says to me, "You're a joiner; you
don't belong to t' Plumbers' Union; this here's a plumber's job.
You keep off it, comrade," he says. Comrade! My God! (*Puts
sugar in tea and pushes sugar basin away.*) But I had to keep off it.

OGLETHORPE. Course you had.

OAKROYD. Well, I were doing nowt again, then, and I saw old
Thorley, t' manager, and he begins talking about some of us older
'uns being worse nor t' young 'uns, idling abart instead o' setting
an example. That was enough for me. (*Puts teaspoon in saucer.*)
I ses summat I shouldn't ha' said——

OGLETHORPE. And you did reight, lad.

OAKROYD. So he says, "Pay him off and give him his card;
he's finished wi' Higden's for good and all." So *I* told him what
he could *do* wi' Higden's.

MRS. OAKROYD. Aaaa, dear, all that comes o' not keeping a
civil tongue in your head, Jess Oakroyd. I've warned you afore
now.

OAKROYD. What d'you think I'm *made* of? When a chap's
called a blackleg i' t' morning an' an idler i' t' afternoon, he's got
to say summat.

OGLETHORPE. And what did you say to him, Jess?

OAKROYD. What? "Oh, you go to hell!" I ses, and marches
out.

OGLETHORPE. And you did reight, lad.

MRS. OAKROYD. Oh, did he? Well, I'm t' best judge o' that,
Sam Oglethorpe. We 'aven't all come into a bit o' money, like you.
(*To* OAKROYD.) And what are you going to do now, then?

OAKROYD (*pushing aside his cup, bitterly*). I don't knaw. Line
up for t' dole till another job turns up. (*He takes out his pipe and
fills it.*)

MRS. OAKROYD. And how long 'ull that be?

OAKROYD. Don't ask me. You knaw what it is nar.

OGLETHORPE (*shaking his head*). Aye, trade's bad i' Bruddersford.

(LEONARD, *who has been standing by the door smoking his cigarette, comes forward to* R. *of* OAKROYD.)

LEONARD. Who says trade's bad ? *I* don't. And if you're out o' work, I know a way we can knock so much off the rent every week !

MRS. OAKROYD (*crossing behind* OAKROYD. *Quickly to* LEONARD). Not now ! Not now ! 'Elp me with the tea-things like a good lad.

(*She hands him the teapot and indicates the scullery.* LEONARD *takes the pot and goes off up* R. *She takes up the other things from the table.*)

OAKROYD (*meanwhile, suspiciously*). What's all this palaverin' behind my back ?

MRS. OAKROYD. Nowt ! Nowt ! Don't you worry your 'ead about that.

(*Exits up* R.)

(*To* LEONARD, *in scullery.*) Tha great gawmless gobbin, what did you want to speak abaht it now for ! (*Slams door.*)

OAKROYD. They're hatchin' summat between 'em. As usual. Thick as thieves. I'm nobbut i' t' way i' my own house. It wor different when our Lily was here. Aa, I do miss t' lass. It's nivver been t' same since her left. I *do* miss her. (*Finishes filling his pipe.*)

OGLETHORPE. I can see that, lad.

OAKROYD. If she'd nobbut say t' word, I'd be off out there, like a shot, I would. But she nivver does. Not a word.

OGLETHORPE. Nay, you'd nivver go to Canada, would yer, Jess ? It's a long way off, and nowt to sup, they tell me, and snaw months and months on end.

OAKROYD. I'll tell tha what it is, Sam. (*Strikes match and lights pipe.*) I've gotten fair sick o' Bruddersford lately. I'd like to knock up and down a bit, and see what there is to see afore I'm too old and daft to tak' onny notice.

OGLETHORPE. Well, tha's been down south once, lad. Tha'd six months theer, i' what's it—Leicester. Tha's seen summat already, Jess.

OAKROYD. Nowt much.

OGLETHORPE. Nay, look at me. I once went for a day to Southport to see t' sea, but I nivver saw it, not a drop. That were a reight take-in, that wor.

OAKROYD. I'd like to go down south again. I'd like to have a look at—oh, well—Bristol. I'd like to see—yer know—some o' *them* places—Bedfordshire.

OGLETHORPE (*shaking his head*). I nivver heard tell much o' that place ; is there owt special i' Bedfordshire, Jess ?

OAKROYD. I don't knaw. But it's summat to see.

(*The room has grown dark.*)

We'll 'ave a bit o' light on t' subject. (*Rises, pushes chair in close to table. Crosses down* L. *and lights the gas by the fire—he sees* ALBERT'S *bag and box.*) Here ! Who's is them ?

OGLETHORPE. I fancy them belongs to " Hello, hello, hello, there ! "

OAKROYD (L.). Hello, there ? (*Steps forward to* L.C.) You don't mean that gurt silly squawking Albert ?

OGLETHORPE. He was 'ere a minute afore you come 'ome.

OAKROYD (L.C.). So that's it, is it ? Comin' 'ere as a lodger, eh ? An' I told 'em, I told 'em. Whose house do they think this is ?

(OGLETHORPE *rises.*)

We'll see about that. (*Picks up bags. Turns and sees* OGLETHORPE *rising and throws bags in corner again.*) You're not off, are yer ?

OGLETHORPE (*goes towards door* R.). Well, I want to see our Ted. He's off down south to-night wi' a load from Merryweather's—on his lorry.

OAKROYD (*staring speculatively*). He is, is he ? To-night, eh ? (*Down* L.C.)

OGLETHORPE. Aye, an' our Ted 'ull give onny friend o' mine a lift onny time. (*Comes* C. *behind table.*) An' I'll tell thee another thing, lad. Thee and me's been mates a long time, and I've had what bit o' luck's been goin' and tha hasn't. Well, there's a pound or two—happen fower or five—here this minute 'at's doing nowt, and tha's only to say t' word and it's thine till tha's ready to pay.

OAKROYD. Thanks, owd lad.

OGLETHORPE (*going to door* R.C.). I'll be off, then, to see our Ted. So if you want me, Jess, you'll knaw where to find me. (*Turns and takes hat from sewing machine,* R., *puts it on.*) Behave thi-sen, lad.

(OGLETHORPE *goes out on to street and turns* L. OAKROYD *goes nearer the fire and stands staring at it.* MRS. OAKROYD *comes out of the scullery up* R. LEONARD *stands in the scullery doorway.*)

MRS. OAKROYD (*behind table* C.). Well, me and Leonard's talked it over—and that settles it.

OAKROYD (L.). What settles what ?

MRS. OAKROYD. Albert comes here.

OAKROYD. Settled that afore, hadn't you ? Nar I've warned you. If Albert comes here, I go.

MRS. OAKROYD. Don't talk so soft. It was bad enough before, but now you've gotten yourself out of work you've no room to talk at all.

OAKROYD. You might ha' let me off this one night, onnyhow. I've had bother enough to-day.

MRS. OAKROYD. It's got to be settled.

OAKROYD. Well,. I've told yer. If he comes, I go.

MRS. OAKROYD (*in a sudden rage*). Well, go then, go on, go on. Go an' live at t' Midland Hotel on your dole money. Go on. Go.

OAKROYD (*crossing towards door down* R.). All right. Say no more. Say no more.

(*He goes off by the door down* R.)

LEONARD (*going down* R.). What's the matter with him, mother ?

MRS. OAKROYD (C.). I don't know and I don't care. You might think they'd just made him manager instead o' stopping him. But it's no good him getting on his high horse now. If he doesn't like Albert being here, he'll ha' to do t'other thing, that's all. My mind's made up. (*Crosses to fireplace* L.)

(ALBERT *puts his head round the* R.C. *door from* R.)

ALBERT. Is it all right ?

MRS. OAKROYD (L.). Yes, course it is. Come in, Albert, an' mak' yourself at home.

(*Enter* ALBERT *with gramophone, which he places on* R. *end of table.*)

ALBERT (C.). That's the style. All merry and bright, eh ? What do you think o' the old gramophone, eh ?

MRS. OAKROYD (L.). Looks nice, Albert. An' we'll be able to have a bit o' music at night.

ALBERT. Have some *now*, if you like. Cheer us all up. The old firm, eh ? There she goes.

(*He starts gramophone and sings, and* LEONARD *joins in. During song* ALBERT *crosses to* R., *leaving* LEONARD R.C. OAKROYD *enters down* R. *He is looking grim and carrying a small basket trunk, which he pitches down on the sofa beside his bag of tools, up* L.C. *Then, with a flick of his finger he sends the needle of the gramophone across the record with a scratch. The gramophone stops.*)

OAKROYD (C. *above table*). Makking yourself at home, aren't yer, Albert ? Are yer stopping here like ?

| MRS. OAKROYD | | | Yes, he is. |
| LEONARD | } (*together*). | { | That's right. |

OAKROYD. Then, I'm off. (*Goes for cap on sofa* L.C.)

LEONARD (C.). Where to ? You can't go like that, pa.

MRS. OAKROYD (L.). Never mind, never mind. Let him go. Trying his tricks. He'll be in a different frame o' mind very soon, when he comes back.

OAKROYD (*up* L.C., *puts cap on*). Yer can do what you like wi' t' place now—it's your own. (*Pointing to money on table.*) There's a week's money there—happen you'll manage.

MRS. OAKROYD (*going up* L. *of* OAKROYD). Manage ! Think we *will* manage.   Nivver better off, thank you.   You've been wanting a lesson for some time.   Go on.   Off you go.

(OAKROYD *prepares to go.*)

LEONARD (*picking up from table and holding out Insurance card*). Here, half a minute, pa.   You'll have to have this.

ALBERT (*up* R.).   That's right.   Must have your Insurance card.

OAKROYD (*taking the card from* LEONARD *and staring at it for a second,* L.C.).   Aye, suppose I owt—— (*Pauses.*)   Oh, to hell wi' t' card.   (*Tears it up and flings the pieces down ; then picks up his bags.*)

ALBERT.   Now you've done it.   You *have* done it now.

(OAKROYD *crosses to door* R.C.)

LEONARD.   Where yer going ?

OAKROYD (*at door*).   Down south.

(*Exits* R.C. *and off to* L.)

(*Triumphant music from the gramophone.*)

BLACK OUT.

SCENE 2

SCENE.—*Front entrance of the Oak and Apple Hotel, Tumbleby.*

TIME.—*Morning.*

A small car is drawn up at L.C. *of door.*   MISS TRANT, *a charming woman of thirty-five, comes out of the hotel,* C.   LANDLORD *is down* L. *below motor-car.*

(*See Photograph of Scene.   Front cloth.*)

LANDLORD (L.).   Your bags are inside the car, Miss Trant.   I think you'll find everything all right.

MISS TRANT (C.).   Thank you.   (*Comes down* C.)

LANDLORD (L.).   You're going to have a nice day for a run. Going far, miss ?

MISS TRANT.   I'm supposed to be going to Liverpool, to see the new cathedral.

LANDLORD.   Tidy way from here to Liverpool.   I did it once.

MISS TRANT.   Do you know the road ?

(LANDLORD *crosses to* R.C.)

(L.C.)   I'm afraid I'm hopeless at maps.   (*Produces map from motor-car seat and places it on bonnet of car.*)   It looks such an awful muddle.   Not that it matters very much.   I'm only wandering about for fun.

LANDLORD (R.C.).   Beg pardon, miss.   But do you think it's

quite safe for a nice lady like you to wander about the country all
by your lonesome ? Don't you think it's a bit risky ?

Miss Trant (c.).   But that's exactly what I'm out for—the risk
—the adventure.   For the first time in my life I'm free of all re-
sponsibilities and—well, I want to see something of the world—
enjoy myself in my own particularly harmless way—somehow.

Landlord.   Well, as long as you don't come to grief, miss.

Miss Trant.   Oh, I shan't come to grief !   In fact, if all the men
I fall in with are no more dangerous than you, I shall be seriously
disappointed.

Landlord.   Well, miss, (*laughing*) I'm afraid I'm a very poor
'and at frightening ladies.

Miss Trant (*laughing*).   I'm afraid so, too.   (*Turning to the map.*)
Now, as to the road——

Landlord.   Now, look here, miss.   (*Comes c. to r. of* Miss
Trant.)   If you make for Melton Mowbray and then take that
turn—(*pointing at place on map*)—you see.

Miss Trant (*pointing*).   You mean, I turn there.   What's the
name of the place ?   Rawsley.

Landlord (*very solemnly*).   That's it.   (*Turns away* r.c.)   And
that's a funny thing, too.   We had a telegram came here, only
yesterday, from that very place.   Came for one of our staff—Effie,
the girl in the bar.   (*Calls her through door* c.)   Effie !   Effeee !

(Miss Trant *goes down* l. *and puts map in car.*)

Effie (*appearing at door* c.).   Did you call, Mr. Bootle ?

(Effie *is a peroxided typical barmaid.   She has a tumbler and glass-
cloth in her hands.*)

Landlord (r.c.).   I was just telling this lady—didn't you get
a telegram yesterday from Rawsley ?

Effie (c.).   Yes, our Elsie sent it.   That's my sister, you know.
She's on the stage.   She's playing at Rawsley with the Dinky Doos.
(*Blows glass.*)

Miss Trant (l.c., *bewildered*).   With the what ?

Effie.   The Dinky Doos.   That's the name of the Concert Party.
Yes, and it's a shame—they're having an awful time—oo, awful.
Are you going that way, miss ?

Miss Trant.   I think so.

Effie (*making a slight move down*).   Well, if you are—I don't like
asking——

Miss Trant.   Why, what is it ?   (*Goes up to* l. *of* Effie.)   Something about your sister ?

Effie.   Yes.   You see, miss, she sent me a telegram yesterday,
asking me to send on her other basket, with her spare costumes in,
y'know.   And it's all right saying " Send it at once," but you've
got to get it there, haven't you ?   I thought if you was going that
way—well——

LANDLORD (R.C., *rather severely*). You've no right to ask, Effie. (*With a broad smile at* MISS TRANT.) But perhaps the lady wouldn't mind ?

EFFIE (C., *wildly*). I wouldn't ask, Mr. Bootle, only I'm sure you understand, don't you, miss ? I know our Elsie's having an awful time, else she wouldn't be wanting her basket. And I know if you took it, she'd get it safe all right.

MISS TRANT (L.C.). Oh, I'll take it, certainly. (*Looking round at car.*) It's not very big, is it ?

EFFIE. Oh no, you'd get it on the back or in the inside easily. I'll go and get it.

(*Hurries indoors,* C.)

LANDLORD (R.C.). She's had her sister on her mind ever since she got that telegram. That's what it's like on the stage, y'know —up this week and down next—here to-day and gone to-morrow. Effie here tried it for a bit, but she's better off where she is and she knows it. When you're behind a bar you do know where you are, don't you ?

MISS TRANT (L.C., *amused*). I don't think I should.

(EFFIE *re-enters* C. *with small theatrical basket.*)

EFFIE (C.). If you wouldn't mind, miss. It's got the name and address on, see ? (*Showing label fixed on basket handle.*) Miss Elsie Longstaff, care of the Dinky Doos, Assembly Rooms, Rawsley.

(*The* LANDLORD *takes the basket from* EFFIE *and crosses and puts it on the back of the car,* L.)

If you wouldn't mind asking for her at the hall there.

MISS TRANT. Very well. (*Comes round to downstage door of car.*) I'd rather like to see the—the Dinky Doos. And you say they're having an awful time ? Poor Dinky Doos.

EFFIE. Thank you ever so much, Miss Trant. And, Miss Trant, when you see our Elsie, will you please tell her I'm writing to her —and would you please give her this ? Tell her it's all I could manage. (*Holds out pound note.*)

MISS TRANT (*down* L.C. *in front of car and taking it and looking first at the note and then at* EFFIE, *then smiling as if rather moved*). I see. Do you always trust strangers—like this ?

(LANDLORD *opens door of car and stands* L.)

EFFIE. No fear. Not me. But—well, you're different. (*Goes into doorway.*)

MISS TRANT. Thank you. (*Gets into car.*) I'll find your sister as soon as I can—though you never know with this car. (*Starts car up.*) Good-bye.

EFFIE.
LANDLORD. } Good-bye.

(*Car goes out* R. *and they look after it.*)

LANDLORD (*going* o.). How did you know what her name was ?
EFFIE (C.). I looked on the label of her bags.
LANDLORD (L.C.). Now then, what about them glasses ?

> (*Exits into hotel as lights fade out.*)

> BLACK OUT.

Scene 3

SCENE.—*The Schoolroom at Washbury Manor School.*

TIME.—*It is late evening, about nine, and the lights are on.*

It is a fairly large, dreary-looking room, the walls covered with old maps, etc., several bookcases filled with school books ; and one small chair ; desks and forms placed near the walls, leaving the o. of the room almost clear. Door up L. Practicable. French window o. To the R., in a prominent position, is an upright piano, of the type used in schools. Window curtains are closed.

(See Photograph of Scene. Large set.)

When the CURTAIN *rises,* INIGO JOLLIFANT, *twenty-three, good-looking, keen, and* FAUNTLEY *are discovered with whisky and soda. Both characters have obviously had some drinks already, but they are not drunk.* FAUNTLEY, *a heavy, middle-aged man, is almost purple in the face and speaks rather too carefully for complete sobriety ; and* INIGO *is rapidly arriving at the hilarious and reckless stage.* INIGO *is seated at the piano playing, a drink before him on the piano.* FAUNTLEY *is sitting o. with legs across chair, with his arms resting on back.*

INIGO (R., *breaking off with a loud chord*). Fauntley ! I haven't had such fun on the piano for weeks ! (*He crashes a few chords in rapid succession.*)

FAUNTLEY (R., *rising*). I wonder what our worthy head, Mr. James Tarvin, and his still worthier spouse, Mrs. Gorgon Tarvin, would say if they could hear you now ? (*Crosses to chair* L.)

INIGO. Well, they can't hear me. (*Chord. Gets up, goes* o.) They're a good safe seven miles away, dining heavily with the vicar. (*Goes up* R., *gets glass from piano and comes down* o.)

FAUNTLEY (*sitting* L.). And may they get stuck on the road coming back and have to spend the night in a ditch ! Cheerio !

> (*They drink.*)

INIGO (o.). She thinks by keeping us on a low diet—to crush our spirits, but she won't succeed. (*Comes over* L. *behind* FAUNTLEY *to desk* L. *with drinks on.*) Do you know, Fauntley, we've had shepherd's pie three times this week and prunes four times——

FAUNTLEY. Have we ? I never notice. I've stopped eating during term.

INIGO (*at desk* L. *of* FAUNTLEY). Quite.

(FAUNTLEY *reaches for bottle.*)

You only drink, Fauntley. No, not just now. (*Takes bottle.*) I'm going to take sandwiches and (*comes* C.) chocolate down and eat them in front of her, right *at* her. (C.) It isn't that I care about food. (*Stands with one foot on chair* C., *with bottle upraised.*) My soul, Fauntley, my soul is like a star and dwells apart—absolutely. (*Drinks, then sits* C.) But I ask you! Can you worthily instruct the young, day after day, on prunes? No, it can't be done, and twenty thousand Cornishmen shall know the reason why. (*Puts bottle down at* R. *side of chair.*)

(*The clock, off* L., *strikes nine.*)

FAUNTLEY. Hello! Nine o'clock? It doesn't look as if your friend is turning up. By the way—who is he?

INIGO (*seated* C.). He's an actor chap I met in the "Red Lion" last night. He struck me as an amusing cove.

FAUNTLEY. D'you think he *will* turn up?

INIGO. There's time yet. He looked as if he'd be glad to turn up anywhere, particularly if there were any free drinks going. I hope he does. I'd love to see him with the Tarvins.

FAUNTLEY (*rising and going* L.C.). Well, Jollifant, having drunk your health several times on this, your twenty-sixth birthday, I will now proceed to give you——

INIGO (C.). Not a present, Fauntley. Don't say you've bought me a present.

FAUNTLEY (L.C.). I will now proceed to give you—a little good advice. Get out of this place. You don't like it, and I don't think it likes you.

INIGO. I'm quite sure it doesn't.

FAUNTLEY. Mind you, whatever you may say about prep. schools, a gentleman can still teach in 'em. Don't forget that. These are the only places left (*hiccough*) for a gentleman.

INIGO. No doubt. But it's pretty ghastly being a (*hiccough*) gentleman, isn't it?

FAUNTLEY. It's nearly played out—like this drink. Pass the bottle, Jollifant.

INIGO. Oh Lord, there you are. It's not at all good for you. (*Passes bottle.*)

FAUNTLEY. It's devilish dry work giving good advice. (*Pours drink into glass.*)

INIGO (*drinks and goes to piano. Putting glass on piano*). It's just as dry taking good advice. (*Sits at piano and plays.*)

FAUNTLEY (C.). You ought to do something with this piano stuff of yours. You're damn clever at it. That thing you were playing just now.

INIGO. Oh, I've got a better one than that. A little thing I was polishing up on Saturday night when the Tarvin woman came in and turfed me out. It's called " Going Home." I finished it this morning. Sit down and see what you think of it. (*He plays " Going Home " chorus.*) *

(*After playing chorus through, he starts it again. And voice is heard off soon after start of second chorus, then a banjo joins in. He begins playing and singing very softly. As he continues, first picking up a few notes, then gradually finding the tune. Then a girl's voice joins in softly.* INIGO *stares at* FAUNTLEY, *then suddenly stops. The banjo stops, too. In the sudden silence that follows, the girl laughs.*)

(R.O.) Gosh! Did you hear that? Come in. (*Goes to* R. *of window and pulls the curtain back.*)

(SUSIE DEAN, *a delightful girl of twenty, enters* O. FAUNTLEY *rises.*)

Oh, I say!

SUSIE (O.). Oh, do you? Good evening.

INIGO. Er—good evening. How d'you do? What a wonderful night—I mean, day—it is—it was—it has been—I mean to say—jolly good of you to come. And—er—how are you?

SUSIE. You mean, who am I? (*Turns round, goes up* O., *calls through window.*) Hurry up, uncle, or they'll think I'm a burglar. (*Comes down* C.)

INIGO (R.O.). We don't care if you are, do we, Fauntley?

FAUNTLEY (R.). Not a bit.

INIGO. If you'd like to burgle, help yourself. Have a map. Have a globe. Help yourself to a desk. Have a drink?

SUSIE (L.O.). No, thanks.

INIGO. Oh, do have something. Do have a drink.

(*Enter* MORTON MITCHAM, *a regular old actor of fifty-five, through window* O. *Comes down* O. *between them.*)

MITCHAM (O.). Certainly, I'll have a drink, my boy. A-ha, here we are, then. Susie, this is my dear old friend—er—Mr.—er—Mr.— er——

INIGO (R.O.). Jollifant, Inigo Jollifant. Ridiculous name, isn't it? How d'you do? (*Shakes hands again enthusiastically, across* MITCHAM.)

MITCHAM (O.). This is my niece, Miss Susie Dean, who's just joined forces with me and is—I don't mind telling you—the most promising little comedienne *in* concert party work or *out* of concert party work to-day. And I'm Morton Mitcham. Twice round the world. Round the world.

(*Passes between them and comes down* R. *to* FAUNTLEY, *who introduces himself and takes him over to chair* L. *for a drink.* MITCHAM *sits in armchair;* FAUNTLEY *on desk.*)

*See note on page 2.

SUSIE (C.). But tell me, where *did* you get that marvellous new number from ?

INIGO (R.C., *puzzled*). Number ?

SUSIE (C.). Yes, number.

INIGO (R.C.). Wait a minute. You don't want me to think of a number and then double it—or anything like that, do you ? I mean—I'll do it—I'll do anything for you—absolutely——

SUSIE (C., *severely*). Are you trying to be funny ? Because if you are, let me tell you—yours is a rotten *act*, and I'm funny for a living and I know.

INIGO. I assure you, Miss Dean, I do assure you——

SUSIE. Oh, stop assuring me. I mean, that number you've just been playing.

INIGO. Oh, that. Simply a little thing of my own. I make them up to amuse myself, you know. You've got to do something in this school, I can tell you. Look at it. (*Waves his hand.*) But did you like it really ?

SUSIE. Loved it. Do you really invent them yourself ? Have you done any more ? Play that one again.

INIGO. I will if you'll sing it for me. I bet you've got a grand voice. (*Goes to piano.*) Look here, there's nobody in ; we can make as much row as we like—this is great fun. Ready ? Right. Here are the words.

(R. *of piano, she reads words of verse to the music, then sings chorus.*)

MITCHAM (*spoken through verse, seated* L., *tapping banjo*). More a little hobby of mine than anything else, you know. This and conjuring. But it's made the evening go, all over the place. Guest nights at Residencies, you know, and that sort of thing. By the way, you're not related to old Sir Elkin Fauntley, by any chance, are you ?

FAUNTLEY (L. *of desk*). Distantly, very distantly. Second cousin —or fourth uncle—something of that sort. Why ? Do you know him ?

MITCHAM. Knew him well in the old days—out East. He was Governor then. Wanted me to give him banjo lessons. "Damn it all, Mitcham," he said to me, "you'll have to teach me to play that thing." "Very proud, Sir Elkin," I told him, "but it can't be done !" "Damn it all," he said, "it must be done !" "It would take years," I told him. "Then you'll have to stay here years," he said. "I'll have you kept here, Mitcham, kept here— damned if I won't !" "Can't be done !" I told him. "I'm catching the next boat up to Bangkok." And he had to give in. Ha, ha, ha !

FAUNTLEY. Ha-ha-ha ! Nobody can say you've not travelled, can they ?

MITCHAM. Three times round the world.

SUSIE (*comes over to* MITCHAM, L.). Never mind about that old gag. Listen to this, uncle. It's a marvellous little number. And he says he's got another one that's better. Listen. I've learned

the words—or most of 'em. (*Goes back to piano. Sings one chorus
" Going Home."*)

(MITCHAM *plays banjo.*)

INIGO (*very excited and happy*). Now you listen to the other
one. I only finished it to-day and it's very roughly written out, so
I'll play you the refrain first just so that you can catch on to the
tune. It's called " Slippin' Round the Corner." (*Gives her the
words and then plays.*) *

(SUSIE *reads the words of the chorus. She reads the final words
" Slippin' round the corner " too soon, and* INIGO *says, " No, no,
that's not it at all," and then sings the last phrase of the chorus
correctly.*)

SUSIE (*enthusiastically, leaning over top of piano*). It's marvellous !
You're completely wasted here. Why don't you come with us ?
INIGO (*rising to* R. *of piano*). Where are you going ?
SUSIE (L. *of piano*). A little place called Rawsley. To join up
with a Concert Party there. They're called the Dinky Doos.
INIGO. The what ? The Dinky Doos ? Oh Lord ! I couldn't
be a Dinky Doo—I should feel a perfect fool all the time—I would
absolutely.
SUSIE. All right, you needn't be highbrow about it. You don't
even know if they'd have you yet. You're only an amateur, you
know—(*imitating him*) absolutely.
INIGO. Shattered !
SUSIE. Let's try it again.

(INIGO *plays a few bars of* " Slippin' Round the Corner." *She sings.*)

INIGO. I say, you're getting awfully good at this. Once more
through and a bit more slowly and you'll know it perfectly. Ready
—go !

(*One verse—one chorus—one dance chorus.* MITCHAM *joins in with
banjo. They are all in good spirits, and work the thing up to a fine
climax. At the height of it, the* TARVINS *enter ;* MRS. TARVIN, *a
tall, commanding figure, first. It is some time before she can make
herself heard.* MRS. TARVIN *enters door* L. *towards end of dance.*
SUSIE *rushes to piano and bangs on the keys to stop* INIGO, R.)

MRS. TARVIN (C., *in a towering rage*). What is the meaning of
this ? What ? What ? And after I'd spoken to you only last
Saturday and told you not to play the piano after hours ! It's an
outrage ! A perfect outrage !

(INIGO *stands on piano-stool with one foot on piano, having closed the
lid.*)

INIGO (*striking an attitude, very dramatically*). " How now, you
secret, black and midnight hag ? "

＊See note on page 2.

MRS. TARVIN (C.). What? What did you say? I've never been so insulted in all my life. The schoolroom a taproom. And who are these people? Why don't you say something? Why don't you say something, James?

(INIGO *comes down below piano* R.)

TARVIN (L.C., *coming forward. He has a slight impediment in his speech*). Yes, certainly, my dear. Disgraceful! You ought to be ashamed of yourself, Jollifant. Really! Really!

MRS. TARVIN (C.). You must leave in the morning. James, he must leave in the morning. I won't have him here a day longer.

TARVIN (L.C.). Rather awkward. Must have a term's notice.

INIGO (*coming* R.C. *to* MRS. TARVIN). Yes, if I leave in the morning, you must pay me a term's salary. Fifty-two pounds. A mere pittance, ladies and gentlemen, but mine own—absolutely.

MRS. TARVIN. I don't care about that. I'll have him out to-morrow whatever it costs me. Give him a cheque, James.

INIGO (R.C.). All right. But I'm *not* leaving in the morning.

MRS. TARVIN. Certainly you are.

INIGO. I'm not. I'm leaving *now*.

MITCHAM (*up stage* R.C.). That's a good line. Hold it.

INIGO (*crosses to* L.). So make that cheque out now, Mr. Tarvin. I'll pack a knapsack. Fauntley, you'll see to the rest of my things, won't you? Tell you later where to send them.

(*He goes out* L., *hurrying*.)

(SUSIE *sits down on chair below piano* R., *and suddenly laughs*.)

MRS. TARVIN. Impudence! I don't know who you are or how you come to be here, but please leave at once. This is a respectable preparatory school and not a—not a——

(TARVIN *exits door* L., *blustering*.)

MITCHAM (R. *of her, drawing himself up with immense dignity, and coming down to* MRS. TARVIN). And not a what, madam? And not a—well, madam, what is it you wish to say? I can hardly believe you know to whom you're talking.

MRS. TARVIN. I don't know and I don't care. (*Turns down* L.C.) Ridiculous!

SUSIE (*rising and going up between* MITCHAM *and* MRS. TARVIN, *confronting her with a marked affectation of great disdain and hauteur, and speaking in an obviously false accent*). How dah you? How dah you speak to us in that mahnar? Obviously you don't in the least know to whom you're talking. This is my uncle—er—Sir——

(*As* MITCHAM *speaks,* SUSIE *goes up* C. *and then* R. *behind piano*.)

MITCHAM (R.C., *with great dignity*). Sir Elkin Pondberry, madam, late Governor-General of Calingapatam, Bimplipatam, and Rajahmundry. (*Strikes chord on banjo.*) A mere hobby, this, my good woman, to pass the time. Ask anybody in any of the Residencies and more exclusive clubs out East. (*He plays a few chords through his lines.*)

MRS. TARVIN (C., *puzzled and uneasy*). I don't believe it.

(FAUNTLEY, *down* L., *gives a guffaw—she turns on him.*)

Mr. Fauntley, you ought to be ashamed of yourself, a master of your experience.

(TARVIN *re-enters door* L. *with the cheque.*)

MITCHAM. One moment, my dear sir. Pardon me.

(*He goes to the puzzled* TARVIN *and produces a trick bunch of flowers, which he hands with a bow to* MRS. TARVIN, *who takes it involuntarily.*)

MRS. TARVIN (R.C.). How dare you! Mountebanks! (*She throws the bunch of flowers up* R.) Leave at once.

(INIGO *re-enters door* L. *He is carrying a knapsack and is wearing a raincoat.*)

INIGO. Have you got my cheque, Mr. Tarvin? (*Receives it.*) Thanks very much. (*Goes down to* FAUNTLEY, L.)

FAUNTLEY (L.). But look here, Jollifant, you young ass, where are you going?

INIGO (L.C.). Well—— (*Turns and looks at* SUSIE.)

MITCHAM (C.). He's going with us. I can see it in his eye. He's a born trouper.

INIGO. Yes, I'm going with you. I'll be a Dinky Doo if it kills me. Fauntley—(*shakes hands*) I'll let you know what happens. Mr. Mitcham, Miss Dean, I'm in your hands. After you.

(*Exeunt* SUSIE *and* MITCHAM, C.)

Good-bye, Tarvin. (*To* MRS. TARVIN.) Madam, your servant.

MRS. TARVIN. Bah!

(*Exit* INIGO, *singing*, C., *following* MITCHAM *and* SUSIE.)

(FAUNTLEY *goes up* C. *with drink in his hand.* TARVIN *stands staring after them.*)

FAUNTLEY (*turns and faces front*). He's a young fool. He's a damned young fool! (*Holds up his hand for silence.*)

(*They hear the sound of the banjo being played softly and retreating;* SUSIE *also singing "Going Home."*)

And if I were twenty years younger, I'd be with him. Here's luck to him. (*Drinks.*)

(*The sound of the banjo grows fainter.*)

BLACK OUT.

SCENE 4

SCENE.—*A country road in the Midlands.*

TIME.—*Late afternoon.*

*A dilapidated motor-van-cum-caravan is drawn up by the roadside, L.
One trestle of a stall is broken and is leaning against another, R.C.
(See Photograph of Scene. Front cloth.)*

When the CURTAIN *rises, its owner,* JOBY JACKSON, *a man of indefinite
age—humorous, keen—is discovered trying to do a bit of carpentering,
sawing wood to mend trestle. He is singing as he works,* C. OAK-
ROYD *enters* L. *and crosses to* R., *carrying his bag of tools and his
little basket trunk, and when he sees* JACKSON, *he stops, puts down
his things, and fills and lights his pipe. He is very dusty.*

JACKSON (C., *looking up and winking*). Nice day, George.

OAKROYD (R.). Aye, nice enough, Herbert.

JACKSON. 'Ere, 'alf a minute. Now I ask you. Do I look like
Herbert ?

OAKROYD. Nay, I don't know. You look as much like Herbert
as I look like George. But I'll tell you what you don't look like.

JACKSON. Go on, George. I'll buy it.

OAKROYD. You don't look like a chap as knows how to use a
saw.

JACKSON. Oh ? Now we're 'earing something, aren't we ? Do
you know all about saws, George ?

OAKROYD. You just tell me what you're trying to do, mate, and
I'll soon show you what I know about saws.

JACKSON. 'Ello, 'ello ! What's the ruddy idea ? You a tradesman, George ? (*Lights Woodbine.*)

OAKROYD. I am an' all. I'm a joiner and carpenter by trade.

JACKSON. Well, I'll tell you something now. My turn, see ?
You don't come from round here. You come from Leeds.

OAKROYD (*turning on him indignantly*). Nay, I don't. I come
from Bruddersford.

JACKSON. Same thing.

OAKROYD. Same thing—nowt ! Leeds is Leeds, and Bruddersford's Bruddersford, and they're as diff'rent as chalk and cheyse.

JACKSON. Near enough. Knew you come from that way. Tell
it in a minute. Bruddersford, eh ? Know Lane End Fair ?

OAKROYD. Tide, you mean. Lane End Tide.

JACKSON. That's right. Call 'em Tides round there, don't they ?

OAKROYD. 'Course I know Lane End Tide. I wish I'd all t'
brass I've spent on t' 'obby horses an' t' swings an' t' coconuts.

JACKSON. I been there many a time. What you doing round
here ? Looking for a job ?

OAKROYD. I am that. An' I'll ha' to get one right sharp an' all.

JACKSON. Like to have a do at my old stall, George ? I'll see you're all right.

OAKROYD. Leave it to me, mate. (*Takes his coat off.*) Let's have a look at t' job.

(JACKSON *hands him the trestle. He examines it and sets to work.*)

JACKSON. What's your name, George ?

OAKROYD (*putting trestle down*). Oakroyd, Jess Oakroyd. (*Takes saw and piece of wood.*)

JACKSON. Mine's Jackson. Joby Jackson. (*Leans on bonnet of car.*) Everybody in this line knows me. You ask 'em—they'll tell you—Joby Jackson. Done everything—boxing shows, circus try-your-luck games—everything. Had shows o' me own, too—you ask anybody—Joby Jackson. Been everywhere. England, Scotland, Wales, Ireland, Isle o' Man, Isle o' Wight—you can't lose me—marvellous.

OAKROYD. Aye, by gow (*hands saw back and gets his own*) you've been on t' road a bit.

(JACKSON *laughs.* OAKROYD *saws wood.*)

JACKSON. You've said it, George. On a steady line now—(*goes to car, puts saw under seat*)—selling 'em something. (*Returns with two dolls.*) Rubber dolls, rubber animals—you blow 'em, see—and there y' are, see. (*Blows one up and lets it squeak.*)

(OAKROYD *blows one and bursts it.*)

Blime ! you'll bust up all my stock.

(*Throws dolls behind seat of car. Squeak of dolls off* L. JACKSON *laughs.*)

OAKROYD. Do you go round i' that ? (*Pointing at car.*)

JACKSON. That's the idea, George. Carry all the stock in it, and the stall.

OAKROYD. Aye, it's had a nasty knock, this has. Here, lad, tak' ho'd o' this a minute.

(*Gives him trestle to hold while he fits the broken piece into it.*)

JACKSON. This is about all I can do. Funny thing, I'm no good with my hands. Sell anything, do the patter, but can't use my hands. Must have been born a ruddy gentleman.

OAKROYD (*as he takes the trestle from* JACKSON *and puts it down on stage*). Aye, maybe. Or you might ha' been born a bit awkward, and that 'ud give same result. (*Kneels down and prepares to nail piece of wood on trestle.*)

JACKSON (*during this* OAKROYD *gets nails and hammer from his tool-bag and repairs trestle*). This has got its nasty knock from a big bloke called Summers. He and me 'ad a row. And I don't mind telling you, George, I 'ope I've ruddy well seen the last of that bloke. He used to be a bit of a fighting man, but trained on booze, and had to chuck it. He's runnin' one of them " Try-your-strength " things now. You know. (*Imitates striking hammer.*)

OAKROYD (*working*). Aye, I see there's been a bit of bother. Well, ho'd on then a minute. It ought to do champion now, nar then——

JACKSON (L.C.). Let's 'ave some Rosie Lee now. I've got it on the boil.

(*He goes behind van* L. *to fetch the tea and is heard singing from back of car.*)

OAKROYD (C.). Shoo'll be as right as ninepence in a minute.

(*He carpenters and* JACKSON *returns with biscuit tin. On it teapot, army mess-tin and thick cup, with condensed milk in open tin with spoon in it.*)

JACKSON (L.C.). 'Ow's this, George ? (*Pours out tea and sits on box* L.C.)

OAKROYD. Champion! And how's this, Herbert ? (*Showing trestle.*)

JACKSON. Fine, George ; you've made a good job of that. (*Gets spoonful of milk and drops it with a blob into mess-tin and cup.*) Seen any football lately, George ?

OAKROYD (R.). Not since I left Bruddersford.

JACKSON. I suppose you follow Bruddersford United.

OAKROYD. Yes. Have you seen 'em ?

JACKSON. Yes. Not much of a team, though.

OAKROYD. Eh ?

JACKSON. No. I saw Everton beat 'em once four nil on their *own* ground.

OAKROYD (*stepping over basket trunk*). Ah ! An' I tell yer they didn't.

JACKSON (L.C.). And I tell you they did.

OAKROYD (R.C.). Nowt o' t' sort. Everton nivver nivver beat Bruddersford United o' t' United's ground, fower nil—nivver nivver i' all thy born days. Nay, lad, you're off your horses theer.

JACKSON (L.C.). Saw 'em myself. Four nil.

OAKROYD. You can't learn me owt about t' United, I've been following 'em too long.

JACKSON. All right—have a cup of tea.

(OAKROYD *sits on trunk,* R.C. *He examines cup which* JACKSON *hands to him.*)

OAKROYD. What's this ? (*Reads.*) Moseley's Coffee Taverns Limited. And who's them when they're at home ?

JACKSON. Souvenir, George.

OAKROYD. I mun tell our Lily about this.

JACKSON. Your Lily ?

OAKROYD. That's my daughter, you know. There were nowt she liked better nor tides and pantymimes and suchlike and she'll be right interested.

JACKSON. What yer going to do now?

OAKROYD. Nay, I don't knaw. I'll ha' to do summat.

JACKSON. Look here, George, why not stay with me till my pal comes back—might be a day, might be a week. I'm going to a little place called Ribsden to-morrow—got a weekly market and a bit of a fair on—and you can give me a hand, see? What say, George?

OAKROYD (*putting cup down*). Here, you're not doing this 'cos I have nowt? No charity business?

JACKSON. Charity my foot! Who do you think I am? Lord Lonsdale? (*Drinks from mess-tin.*)

OAKROYD (*shaking hands*). Well, I'll be right glad to stay with you till your mate comes back.

JACKSON. Right you are, George, now what about a drop more Rosie?

OAKROYD. No, thanks, lad.

JACKSON. We'd p'raps better be supping it up and hopping along, eh? We've a long way to go before dark. You might help me shove these things in the old van. (*Rises.*)

OAKROYD. What! These trestles?

JACKSON. Yes.

OAKROYD. Shall I shove 'em in the back? (*Goes above car to the back,* L.)

JACKSON. That's right, boy. There's a boozer about two miles down the road, we'll go along and have a can or two. (*Packs tea-things in box and takes them below car to the back,* L.)

OAKROYD. Champion! (*Puts things in van and crosses to* R.) I wanted to go on t' road, and, by gow—I'm on it now and no mistake. (*As he crosses to* R. *for basket and tools.*)

JACKSON (*coming to front of car, taking his coat off the bonnet, and speaking as he starts to crank up*). But you're wrong, George, you're wrong. Bruddersford United—nil. Everton—four. See it with my own eyes.

OAKROYD. You nivver did, lad. T' United lost to Everton one time three nil, but nivver fower—and yer nivver in your life saw it happen. She's a bad un to start. Can I give her a turn?

JACKSON. It's all right. She goes for me sometimes. That's got her.

(*Engine starts with a horrible tinny sound.*)

Get in, George, and let's get off. (*Gets in driver's seat.*)

OAKROYD (*getting in the front*). Aye, before she changes her mind.

(*The van leaves the stage. Pistol shots are fired off* L. *as car moves off* R.)

BLACK OUT.

SCENE 5

SCENE.—*Market-place in Ribsden.*

TIME.—*Afternoon.*

At the back is an inn, " The Helping Hand." The stage is full of stalls, etc. JACKSON'S *stall, covered with notices :* " Joby Jackson is here again—the old firm. Don't forget the little Ones. British Workmanship can't be Beat " *is in the* C., *in front. On the* L. *is a* MAN WITH LINOLEUM, *who has an* ASSISTANT. *On the* R. *is the* PROFESSOR, *and on the* R. *of him, the* MAN WITH THE ENVELOPES. *People are moving about all the time, and among them a large* POLICE-MAN *with a ginger moustache is conspicuous.*
    (*See Photograph of Scene. Large set.*)

When the CURTAIN *rises* JACKSON *and* OAKROYD *are just finishing setting out the rubber toys on the stall ; and the* PROFESSOR, *a tall, seedy man in an old frock coat, with hat and a grey mop of hair, is hanging notices on an easel :* " Do you know your Fate ? Professor Miro can tell you. What is the Message of the Stars ? Destiny —Will Power—Personality. The Chance of a Lifetime. Don't miss it." *There are not many people about at first, but they soon collect round the* LINOLEUM MAN *on the* L., *and the* ENVELOPE MAN *on the* R., *leaving the space in front of* JACKSON'S *stall and the* PROFESSOR *quite clear.*
    Groups talk as the crowd first assemble.

MIDDLE-AGED WOMAN (*to another*). And so I told him, " If you can get 'em in the market here for three and sixpence, why can't you sell 'em ? " He says, " They're not as good."
    SECOND WOMAN. They are. They're every bit as good.
    GIRL (*to* OTHER GIRL). " Well, go to the pictures by yourself next time," I says. " Temper," he says.
    OTHER GIRL. Ooo, look, I believe there's some of them imitation silk stockin's over there, same as Mabel bought, for one and three——
    GIRL. " No temper about it," I says. " Only when I come out," I says, " I don't like to make a show of myself," I says.
    YOUTH (*to* OTHER YOUTH). Well, if a bus like that isn't worth twenty quid, what is it worth ? I call it a snip.
    OTHER YOUTH. Ar, but you want to be careful, see ? Get taken in so easy. No second-hand touches for me. I shall get a new one. Hello, look, who's over there ?
    OLD FARMER (*crossing front of stall* C. *from* R. *to* L. *To* YOUNG FARMER). You don't see beasts like them nowadays, Tom.
    YOUNG FARMER. Oh ! I don't know.
    OLD FARMER. 'Cos you're not old enough, you see. I've seen

the time when beasts were bought and sold in this market-place
that would fetch prizes now, big prizes.

POLICEMAN (*coming from* L.). Morning, Mr. Carey.

OLD FARMER. Ah! William, on the job, eh?

POLICEMAN. Got to be on the job, Mr. Carey. Got some strange
people in the town; some from Doncaster.

OLD FARMER. Well, you're the man for the job.

POLICEMAN. I'll do my best, Mr. Carey.

JACKSON (R.C.). Don't forget the patter. All guaranteed not
to burst, tear, burn, or drown; made of the finest rubber on the
market to-day. Ninepence, one shilling, one-and-six, two shillings;
pick where you like; they're all the very best. That's the stuff,
see?

OAKROYD (C.). Ah, I'll have to do at it later on.

HARASSED MOTHER (*to* SMALL BOY *or* GIRL, *crossing front of stall*
C. *from* L. *to* R.). What d'you want a balloon for? You're too old
for balloons. Besides, if you think I've come here to buy things
for you, you're mistaken. And what was it your father said he
wanted? Bothering me. Oh, come al—on—ng . . .

JACKSON (R.C., *shouting*). Nar then, lady, take yer choice. Ninepence, one shilling, one-and-six, two shillings, all guaranteed not
to burst, tear, burn, or drown, the best rubber on the market.

OAKROYD (*trying his hand at it and not being very convincing*).
That's right. Pick where yer like, missis, they're all t' best.

(*By this time there should be a crowd round the* LINOLEUM MERCHANT,
*who stands on a box and now bursts into speech that the audience
can hear. While he is shouting,* JACKSON *and* OAKROYD *sell toys
and conduct conversation in dumb show. The* PROFESSOR *takes
up a position near his easel, and can if possible do a little comic
business, staring at a small boy or two, standing in front of him.
It is during this period that any extra business, to suggest the life,
colour and movement of an open market and small fair can be inter-
polated.* ENVELOPE MAN *enters from up* R. *and takes up position
down* R.)

LINOLEUM MAN (*banging rolls of lino, shouting himself hoarse*).
Now I'll tell you whattam going ter do, people. Just to make a
start. 'Ere, 'ere, now listen to this, just listen to this. I'm not
going to sell yer linoleum, I'm going to give it yer—here y'are.
Number One. (*Unrolls lino and bangs it.*) Now that's not oilcloth.
I don't sell oilcloth, people. That's the very best lino—carpet
pattern, rubber backed—and yer can't wear it away. Just look
at it. That's lino, *lino*—it isn't oilcloth. (*Bangs it.*) Five shillings.
(*Bang.*) Four and six. (*Bang.*) Four shillings. Well, I'll tell
yer what I'll do, people. Three and six. Three and six, and I'm
giving it away. (*Carries on, but in dumb show.*)

ENVELOPE MAN (*on the* PROFESSOR'S R. *He is very carefully
dressed, spectacles, and roars with great solemnity holding up a mys-*

terious envelope). And when Mis-ter Wal-ters of Bris-tol gave me these envelopes, he assured me that in every one of them there was a bank-note. Mr. Wal-ters sent me down here to sell them to you purely and simply as an advertisement. And when Mr. Wal-ters of Bris-tol guaranteed that there was a bank-note in every one of these envelopes, that was good enough for me, people, for I know Mr. Wal-ters and I knew that Mr. Wal-ters would not send me down here on a fool's errand. But wait a minute—wait a minute, people. There is something else I want to show you. (*Dives down and then reappears holding up small package, then continues in dumb show*.)

LINOLEUM MAN *(with a tremendous outburst, banging away at another piece*). There's three yards here—yer could cover a landing with it and it 'ud last yer a lifetime. And I'll tell you why, people, because it's the very best rubber-backed, carpet-pattern lino ; there isn't any better made anywhere, and you can go where you like to try and find it. It's not oilcloth. I don't sell oilcloth. It's lino. And I'll tell you what I'll do, just to make a start. I'll put the two together—four yards there and three yards here, the very best——

(ENVELOPE MAN *commences*.)

—and you can have the two—not for ten shillings, not for nine shillings, not for eight shillings, and not for seven shillings, but for six shillings. Six shillings the two—and it's not oilcloth I'm trying to sell yer ; it's not oilcloth ; it's the very best lino. . . .

ENVELOPE MAN *(holding up mysterious package*). Oh yes, my friend, I know what's inside here. I know what's inside this package, people. But I'm not going to tell you. I'm going to see if any lady or gentleman has got the pluck, has got the courage, to offer me one shilling—one *silver* shilling—for the article inside this paper. Who's got the pluck ? One shilling—that's all I ask—one silver shilling. You won't regret it.

(ENVELOPE MAN, JACKSON *and* LINOLEUM MAN *start together*.)

ENVELOPE MAN. When Master Wal-ters of Bris-tol sent me down here, he didn't send me down here to make money. I'm not here to make money. I'm simply here to advertise. Now, my friends, I'll show you what I'm prepared to do for you. . . . (*Gets down*.)

JACKSON (*starts his first speech*). All guaranteed not to burst, *etc*.

LINOLEUM MAN (*starts his first speech*). 'Ere, 'ere, now listen to this, *etc*.

(BELLMAN *rings his bell on rostrum* L. *at same cue, when* LINOLEUM MAN *says,* " 'Ere, 'ere, now listen to this." *After ringing bell he comes down* L., *passes in front of* LINOLEUM MAN *and goes up* L. *of stall* C.)

OAKROYD. Well, I don't know.

TOWN CRIER (*ringing bell, up* c.). Oh yez! Oh yez! Oh yez! Lost a watch—this morning—between the hours of nine and eleven —near St. Mary's Church—Five pounds reward. God save the King.

(*He exits up* L. *and rings again when well off stage.*)

(PROFESSOR *approaches and says something.*)

JACKSON. What, going to have one? You come with me, Professor. Here, George, you can look after the stall for a bit, can't you?

OAKROYD. Aye, I'll have a pop at it.

JACKSON. That's the stuff, George. And don't forget them crocodiles is two bob each—they're extra special, they are—they cost *me* ninepence.

OAKROYD. Well, there's nowt like a fair profit. I'll see to t' crocodiles, lad.

(JACKSON *and the* PROFESSOR *go out* R.)

(OAKROYD *is left in charge of the stall. He addresses the* OLD FARMER, *who, being offered a rubber doll or animal, fussily rejects it.*)

Like a rubber duck?

OLD FARMER. No. (*Crosses in front of stall from* L. *to* R.)

OAKROYD. All right, mister, if you'd rather keep your brass i' your pocket. We can't all be spendin', can we?

(SUMMERS, *a big fellow, wearing an old black and red football jersey and a scarf, comes up and stares at the stall and at* OAKROYD, L.C.)

OAKROYD (c., *uneasily*). Like a doll, mate?

SUMMERS (L.C.). Like a doll! Do I look as if I wanted a ruddy doll? Do I now? Do I? Where's that flaming little swine, Joby Jackson? Where is he? D'you 'ear?

OAKROYD (c., *very uneasily*). He's not here.

SUMMERS. Can't I see he's not here? I'm asking where he is. Yer not a ruddy stuck pig, are yer? Yer can talk, can't yer?

OAKROYD. Joby Jackson's not here.

SUMMERS. Ar d'yer mean he's not here? This is his stall, isn't it? Think I don't know it?

OAKROYD (*in despair*). Ay, but—you see—I've bowt it off on him.

SUMMERS. Oh, since when?

OAKROYD. Yesterday.

SUMMERS. He's been seen here this morning. You bought this? You've 'ell as like, you rotten little liar.

POLICEMAN (*the one with the ginger moustache, who appears* R.C. *round the corner at this moment*). Here, here, here, here. Less of it. Less of it. What's all this about?

(*The* PROFESSOR *re-enters* R.)

SUMMERS (*growling*). I come 'ere asking for a feller and this feller says this stall here is his and I was telling him it wasn't—see ?

POLICEMAN (*crossing* OAKROYD *to* C.). Well, I don't see what you've got to make such a lot of noise about.

SUMMERS (L.C., *sulkily*). I was only telling him it wasn't, see ?

POLICEMAN (C., *angrily*). All right, all right, I know what you was doing. And I say it don't seem to me to be much of your business.

OAKROYD (R.C., *eagerly*). That's right. That's right.

POLICEMAN (*turning to* OAKROYD). Oh, is it right ?

(*As* POLICEMAN *turns on* OAKROYD, OAKROYD *steps back and bumps into* PROFESSOR, *who in turn bumps into* OLD FARMER.)

It may be none of his business, but it's my business all right. Now, you say this here outfit belongs to you and not to this other feller he's talking about ?

OAKROYD (*hesitating*). Aye. In a manner o' speaking, as you might say——

POLICEMAN. What d'you mean in a manner o' speaking ? Here, let's have a look at your licence.

OAKROYD (*who obviously has no licence and knows nothing about one*). Well, you see—ay—well—— (*Rubs his chin.*)

SUMMERS (*triumphantly*). He's got no licence.

(OAKROYD *turns to* PROFESSOR *and asks him where* JACKSON *is.*)

POLICEMAN (*angrily*). Who's talking to you. (*Giving him a push.*) You get back a bit.

SUMMERS. And who the hell d'you think you are ? Touch me again, you ginger pic, and I'll flatten you.

(*Enter* JACKSON *from* R.)

POLICEMAN. Another word, another word from you, and you'll come along with me.

JACKSON (*coming* R.C.). Hello, hello, what's the row ?

SUMMERS (*roaring*). There you are !

(*Makes a rush at* JACKSON *and knocks him down.*)

POLICEMAN. Here, here, here, stop that—*etc.*

(*They begin fighting and struggling round the stall, and immediately a crowd collects and there is a great commotion. It is impossible to see exactly what is happening but the stall obviously suffers badly. The* POLICEMAN, *in the thick of it, blows his whistle, and this brings two other* POLICEMEN *on the scene. One from* R. *and one from* L.)

JACKSON'S VOICE (*from the fight—shouting*). You 'op it, George.
OAKROYD (*joining in*). Nay, I'll be damned if I do.

(*The crowd gets larger and larger. The stalls are pushed upstage to
clear for next scene. As the fight starts, LINOLEUM MAN and
ENVELOPE MAN start their patter over again and continue till finish.*)

MUSIC AND BLACK OUT.

SCENE 6

SCENE.—*A wayside road in the Midlands.*

TIME.—*Afternoon.*

MISS TRANT'S car *is drawn up* C. *by the side of the road, with the
bonnet lifted up.* OAKROYD'S *bag of tools and little basket are on
the ground a little in front of the car,* R. OAKROYD *has his head in
bonnet of car and is cleaning a plug, and* MISS TRANT *is sitting in
passenger-seat of car, with her face turned towards him.*

(*See Photograph of Scene. Front cloth.*)

OAKROYD (*lifting his head from inside bonnet*). And then there
wor a fight.

MISS TRANT. A fight?

OAKROYD (*busy with the plug*). By gow—there wor a fight an'
all. I can feel some of it yet. But don't think that's why I left
him. After this gurt madman, Summers, had been takken t' police
station and we wor cleanin' up a bit, this chap Joby's pal turned
up, and so it wor " Finish " for me, d'you see, miss?

MISS TRANT. I see. And what are you going to do now?

OAKROYD. Nar, you're askin' me summat. I don't fairly know.
I thowt I'd have a look at this Rawsley place 'at Joby mentioned.
It's nobbut just down t' road, I fancy.

MISS TRANT. I know it is. That's where I'm going—that is, if
this wretched car hasn't stopped for ever.

OAKROYD. Well, I think it's these mucky plugs 'at's done it.
I've seen 'em do this wi' t' lorries at t' mill——

(MISS TRANT *gets out of car.*)

—you know. Onnyhow, we'll see in a minute.

MISS TRANT (*putting on leather coat*). It's very good of you to
take all this trouble. It's stupid of me, but I don't know anything
about the inside of cars. You must tell me after what I owe you
for this work.

OAKROYD. Nay, miss, you're welcome to it. I'm a carpenter by
trade. This is only a side-line, as you might say, and we're both
on t' road, aren't we? And when folks is on t' road, it's only fair
they should be pally-like.

MISS TRANT. It's nice of you to put it in that way, (*picks up gloves out of car and puts them on*) and I'm sure you're quite right. That's what the rule of the road really means, I should say : friendliness, give and take. And I imagine that's what it always has been, from this moment, when you've come to *my* rescue, right back to the days when knights errant came to the rescue of damsels in distress.

OAKROYD. Nay, I can't say as I know much about them owden times. (*Goes to front of car.*)

MISS TRANT. Well, I do happen to know about them ; I've always read about them, and been thrilled about them. You mightn't think so to look at me. I know my people at home never did—when they saw me sitting solemnly behind a book, they thought I was just reading, but I wasn't, at all ! I was marching by the side of Red Gauntlet, or carrying secret messages from Louis XI to Charles of Burgundy, or with Napoleon thundering over the Rhine, or clattering down the Great North Road to hammer on tavern doors on black nights of wind and storm.

(*Start check of lights.*)

OAKROYD. Well . . . I don't know !

MISS TRANT (*startled*). But for that, I don't believe I should ever have set out when I found myself free. It's the romantic spirit in us, I suppose—or is it just business that brings you on the road ?

OAKROYD. Business ? Nay, I've—er—just taken me hook—yer know—run away from home.

MISS TRANT. Well, there you are ! So have I.

OAKROYD. I nobbut set off o' Monday night. And—by gow—it seems like months sin' I wor i' Bruddersford, I've done so much i' three days. I'm fair capped wi' me-sen. It's like these chaps on t' pictures.

MISS TRANT (*laughing*). That's just what I feel, It's fun, isn't it ? (*Turns away to* L.)

OAKROYD. Aye, up to a point it is. But I can see it mightn't be so funny like—later on.

MISS TRANT. Now, don't let us anticipate trouble. (*Turns back again.*) You must tell me some more of your adventures. But tell me your name first. (*Takes motor tools and puts them on floor of car.*)

OAKROYD (R.C.). Oakroyd—Jess Oakroyd. It's a right owd Bruddersford name.

(*Lightning.*)

MISS TRANT (L.C.). And mine's Trant, and that's an old name too, in Gloucestershire.

(*Thunder.*)

And we're both on the road, as you say.

OAKROYD (*looking up*). Aye, an' it looks like bein' a wet road an' all in a minute. I'll have to hurry up wi' this job. But I think this might do. (*Puts plug in and closes bonnet.*)

MISS TRANT (*as stage darkens*). Yes, it's going to rain. I felt a spot then. (*Moves to rear of car and looks round and sees the lightning which is* R.)

(*Lightning.*)

OAKROYD (*down* C.). I'll——

(*Thunder.*)

—put up the 'ood, shall I ?

(MISS TRANT *goes above car and they put hood up.*)

Well, we'll try her now. Just turn her on.

(MISS TRANT *gets into car, and* OAKROYD *cranks her up. The car starts, but not loudly.*)

(R.C.) She'll do champion now. Well, good day to you, miss. (*Turns away* R.)

MISS TRANT (*leaning her head out*). Yes, but you're coming in, too. Hurry up, Mr. Oakroyd.

(OAKROYD *picks up his things.*)

OAKROYD. I don't mind if I do. Thank you, miss. We'll ha' my basket in t' first, else all my clean clothes'll be sopping wet an' that'll be a poor do. Them first, and me after, an' off we go. (*He puts basket and tools behind seat.*)

(OAKROYD *climbs in, and the car moves off. Fork lightning is seen and a big crash of thunder is heard.*)

BLACK OUT.

SCENE 7

SCENE.—*On the stage of the Assembly Rooms, Rawsley, from the auditorium.*

In the foreground rows of stalls. An entrance to the hall L. *It is a cheap, neglected place.*

(*See Photograph of Scene Large set.*)

JOE BRUNDIT, *fifty ;* MRS. JOE BRUNDIT, *forty-five ;* ELSIE LONG-STAFF, *twenty-three ;* JERRY JERNINGHAM, *twenty-two ;* and JIMMY NUNN, *forty ; are discovered—all talking at once.* ELSIE *is on her knees packing a basket,* R.C. *on stage ;* JERRY *is seated on*

top of steps R. MRS. JOE *seated on basket* L.C. JOE *on basket* L.
JIMMY *on chair below stage* C.
Following lines spoken together as scene opens.

MRS. JOE. It's perfectly ridiculous, we go on arguing and
arguing and never get any further. We go round and round in
a circle. I wasn't blaming anybody, I merely said it would have
been better to make more careful inquiries and then perhaps we
might not have found ourselves in this position.

ELSIE. Oh! shut up! I'm absolutely fed up to the back
teeth with the whole bally show. What's the use of talking?

JERRY (*with an effected drawl*). I'm sick of the whole business;
we're broke, and that's all there is to it. We're in this mess and
we've got to get out of it somehow, so shut up, Elsie.

JOE. I told you when I saw him at the station with her, I
knew what he was going to do—anyhow, what did I say? No
more than I'd have said to you or anyone else. Anyhow—I'm
saying no more about it.

MRS. JOE. No, you said enough last night. The language he
used when he found out!

JOE (*rising and going* L.). Yes, and I'd use some more if I could
get hold of that blasted beast! Letting us all in like this. And all
because of that rotten pianist-woman.

MRS. JOE. Don't call that woman a pianist. If she's a pianist
then I'm the champion tightrope walker.

JERRY. That's all very well, but what's going to herppen to
the poor old Dinky Doos?

NUNN. We're broke to the wide.

ELSIE (*kneeling*). Five months of consecutive work and now I
can't even pay for this week's lodgings. I told that damn landlady
of mine that I'd written to my sister to help me out. But d'you
think the old cat would believe me? Not she! Talked about
"attaching my box."

NUNN. I warned you against going to Ma Maunders.

JERRY. The mingy old skinflint.

ELSIE (*kneeling and packing basket*). Anyhow, I got even with
her. Managed to smuggle my things out bit by bit. There'll be
a hell of a row when she finds my box is empty.

MRS. JOE. I can't bear it! It's beyond human endurance.

JOE (*patting her on the back*). Never mind, old girl——

MRS. JOE. Not "old girl." Don't be vulgar, Joe. This is no
time to be vulgar.

ELSIE (R.C., *rising and turning to* MRS. JOE). Isn't it, my
dear? Well—my God—all I can say is—if there ever was
a dud town or overgrown village or human dog-kennel, it's this
Rawsley.

(*All start talking at once. Dialogue all spoken together.*)

ELSIE. It's just like a rotten manager like Mildenhall to have
gone and done the dirty on us in a place like this.

MRS. JOE. The moment I set eyes on the place I said to myself
—this is not going to be a lucky date for us at all. This is going
to be a bad date.

JOE. What are you leading off for ? It's not Jimmy's fault.
He didn't bring us here, don't open your mouth too wide.

JERRY (*rising and walking to* ELSIE *and back to* R.). Oh, shut up,
Elsie—shouting won't help us.

NUNN (*rising to stop the row*). Now then, boys and girls, we've
stuck it so far, now let's see it through. (*Has been consulting a little
note-book.*) *I've* been trying to work it out, and the first thing is
we owe the people here at the Assembly rooms fifteen pounds, four
and something—and I'll tell you how I work that out——

JERRY (R.). Oh, no, Jimmy, not again.

ELSIE (R.C.). Put that note-book away, Jimmy, for the love of
Mike. Hello, who's this ?

(SUSIE, INIGO *and* MITCHAM *enter up* R. *The latter is carrying his
banjo.*)

NUNN (C., *shouting*). Susie ! Susie Dean ! It is. Is it ? It
is !

SUSIE (*running to him down to front of stage and embracing him*).
Jimmy Nunn. Dear old Jimmy.

NUNN (C., *below*). Well, well, well. I haven't seen you, Susie,
since we was in the Larks and Owls together at Hastings.

(*See Plan* 1.)

You know the rest of us, don't you, Susie ? Here's Joe and Mrs.
Joe. You remember them ?

(NUNN *runs up steps* R. *and comes* C. *behind* SUSIE.)

SUSIE (*turning to them*). 'Course I do. You were in the Pom-
Pom Parade at Hastings, weren't you ?

(MITCHAM *goes* L. *to* JOE.)

MRS. JOE. That's right, dear. That was the time Joe fell
through the stage in a sketch.

JOE. It was. And it was the only time I ever heard that sketch
get a laugh.

(*See Plan* 2.)

JERRY (*stepping forward*). Hello, Miss Dean. How err you ?
(*Shakes hands.*)

SUSIE (C.). Jerry Jerningham, too. My word ! You've got *all*
the talent. (*Turns.*) And this is Mr. Inigo Jollifant, everybody,
who's only an amateur so far, but is almost too clever to live.

(INIGO *comes down* C.)

(*The following dialogue all together as they shake hands with each other.*)

INIGO. Not nearly as clever as you, anyhow.

MRS. JOE (*shaking hands with* INIGO). You sing? Tenor, I presume?

INIGO. I play the piano and try to write songs.

SUSIE. And the most perfect songs, believe me.

MRS. JOE. Indeed! How very gifted! (*Sits* L.C.)

JOE (L.). Mitcham, old boy. D'you remember the old days when we played in the Royal Divorce?

MITCHAM (L.C.). And a damn good Napoleon I was, too. Jehosephine! Jehosephine!

SUSIE (*emerging from group*, C.). But what's happened? Where's Mildenhall?

MRS. JOE (L.C.). Our dear manager has vanished.

SUSIE. Gone?

NUNN (*comes down* L. *of* SUSIE). We're dished, Susie. We're broke.

SUSIE. Oh, my hat! You poor darlings. But what happened?

MRS. JOE (L.C.). Tell her, Jimmy. I haven't the heart. (*Crosses* L. *and sits* L.C.)

(*See Plan* 3.)

NUNN (C.). Mildenhall ran away with the pianist.

ELSIE (R.C.). She was the world's worst performer, my dear. Couldn't have looked little Nellie's instruction book in the face. She called herself Miss Maidstone—after the jail.

NUNN. And that's where she'll end, too. They took the entire treasury with them. We're completely in the potage. Finish. The Dinky Doos. (*Sits on basket* L.C.)

SUSIE. Oh, I say—I am sorry. I mean, not just for our sake, but for yours.

MITCHAM (*comes behind* MRS. JOE *and puts hand on* NUNN'S *shoulder*). Tough—very tough.

NUNN. All my fault too. (*On corner of basket* L.C.)

ELSIE.
MRS. JOE. } It wasn't. Course it wasn't. Don't be silly,
JOE.   } Jimmy.
JERRY.

NUNN. I ought to have known. I'd heard one or two queer things about Charlie Mildenhall.

MITCHAM. You can never tell, old man, never tell. I made the same mistake with an Australian tour in nineteen hundred and eight. And they left us stranded at Brisbane—Brisbane, mark you —a thousand miles from anywhere.

MRS. JOE. Well, I'm sure this place feels as if it's a thousand miles from anywhere.

ELSIE. It *is* a thousand miles from anywhere. And I wish to God I'd never set eyes on it. (*Sits on basket* R.C.)

(*See Plan 4.*)

SUSIE (C.). Can't we *do* something ?

JOE (L.). That's just what I say, Susie.

MRS. JOE. Don't be silly, Joe. You know very well you never say a thing. You only talk. (*Still seated* L.C.)

INIGO (*comes down* C.). I can't be a Dinky Doo then ? Not even after making up my mind to be a Dinky Doo. Well, what happens now ?

NUNN, etc. (*shaking heads*). I dunno. I give it up.

(INIGO *steps back.*)

ELSIE. When I get some money I'm going home and finding a job behind the nearest decent bar. I'm through with the stage. I like to eat when I'm working. I'm through.

SUSIE (C.). Well, I'm not. I'm sticking it. Nothing or nobody's going to make me leave the profession. Some day you'll see little Susie's name in electric lights in Shaftesbury Avenue.

INIGO (*comes down* R. *of* SUSIE). That's the stuff, absolutely.

SUSIE. You be quiet, Professor. You know nothing about it. You're only an amateur. But I say—let's stick it, boys and girls. The luck may turn yet.

(*At this moment* MISS TRANT *enters by door* L. *below, rather hesitatingly, and all of them turn and look at her.*)

MISS TRANT (L.). Is Miss Elsie Longstaff here ?

ELSIE (*coming forward*). That's me.

MISS TRANT. I've a message from your sister. I met her accidentally. And I've a basket for you, too. It's in my car outside.

ELSIE (*she comes down steps* L.). Thank God for that. Do you mind leading me to it, please, before we do anything else ?

(*They go out together, door* L.)

SUSIE (C.). And that's that. Just for a minute I thought we were going to be treated to a bit of magic. You know—enter the Fairy Queen. (*Imitating pantomime style.*)

> Hold, sir, while I display my magic power
> And golden gifts upon you shower !

(*Falls into arms of* MRS. JOE.)

MRS. JOE (L.C.). Don't talk to me of Fairy Queens. Dozens of 'em I've played to Joe's Demon.

(JOE *strikes a dramatic attitude and says* " Ah ! Ah ! ")

Jerry (*coming forward*). Susie, I've just worked out a new dance. It's good, isn't it, Jimmy?

(Mrs. Joe *crosses and goes down to piano down steps*, R.)

Nunn (*solemnly*). It is. It's *good*.

Susie. Let's have a look at it. Go on, cheer us up a bit.

(Joe *and* Nunn *push baskets* L. *up stage and sit on them.* Mitcham *pushes those* R. *up stage and sits* L.C.)

Jerry. All right. You give us the tune, Mrs. Joe. That's it Keep it going.

(*See Plan* 5 *for positions during dance.*)

(Mrs. Joe *plays the piano.* Inigo *and* Susie *go down and sit in front row of seats, and go on up stage again after the dance.* Jerry *does a very clever step-dance. Just before he finishes,* Miss Trant *and* Elsie, *with* Mr. Oakroyd *behind them, come in, and stand watching near the door* L. *At the end of the dance they all applaud.* Mrs. Joe *also goes up on stage.*)

Elsie (*to* Miss Trant). That was clever, wasn't it?

Miss Trant. It was. I loved it.

Oakroyd (*coming forward, puts* Elsie's *basket on stage* L.C. *as he speaks*). It wor champion, that, wat I saw of it. An' I haven't seen owt as good, i' t' same line, at t' Imperial i' Bruddersford, not for a long, long time, I haven't. And I know what I'm talking about, 'cos when I wor a lad I could do a bit i' t' same line me-sen —clog-dancin' style. (*Does a few steps—then to* Jerry.) Champion, lad. Champion! (*Crosses and sits on piano stool,* R.)

(Jerry, Susie *and* Inigo *exit,* R. *on the stage.*)

Elsie (*beckoning* Nunn, *who comes down steps* R., *and comes forward with* Miss Trant). This is Jimmy Nunn, our comedian, Miss Trant, and he can tell you *more* about the show. I've been telling Miss Trant about it, Jimmy.

(*See Plan* 6.)

(*During this dialogue,* Mitcham *sits on* Elsie's *basket,* L.C. Joe *pulls down the other two baskets, and* Mrs. Joe *and* Joe *sit.* Mrs. Joe *winds wool.*)

Miss Trant. How do you do? (*Sits end seat,* L. *of down stage row of chairs.*)

Nunn. Pleased to meet you, Miss Trant. Not in the profession yourself, Miss Trant? No, I thought not, though I used to know a Miss Trant on the MacNaughton Circuit. Trant's Merry Chicks— juveniles, you know—none of 'em over thirty! You're not in management, by any chance, are you?

MISS TRANT. I've never managed anything except a house.

NUNN (*sits end seat of up-stage row of chairs,* L.). Believe me, if you can manage a house as it ought to be managed, you can manage anything. I *know.* I've been living in digs for twenty-odd years—more—and what's the result? I'll tell you. I haven't any digestion left. That's right. Got a wicked stomach—won't look at a thing. Bacon, eggs, ham, chops, steak and chips, bit o' pie—anything you really fancy, y' know—can't touch 'em!

MISS TRANT. What a shame!

NUNN. I haven't had a square meal for three years. And I've got to be *funny.* What a life!

ELSIE. Jimmy! (*Kicks* JIMMY *on his ankle.*) Miss Trant was asking me what we're in the soup for, and what it would take to run the show.

NUNN. Now I've got figures in this (*produces note-book*)—in black and white.

MISS TRANT. You've had a lot of experience, haven't you, Mr. Nunn?

(ELSIE *goes up steps* L. *and joins* MRS. JOE, *etc.*)

NUNN. That's right. A lot of experience. Concert-party work, panto, low comedy in legit!—know it all. And I don't mind telling you that we had the makings of a very good little show here, a very good little show. If only I'd kept an eye on that manager: to think that with all the years I've been on the stage I shouldn't have seen through his game. I tell you what, Miss What's-it, I can't look these boys and girls in the face. (*Groans.*)

ELSIE (*from the group at the back*). There's Jimmy going on again.

(JOE *rises and goes down steps* L. ELSIE *takes his seat.*)

JOE (*coming forward*). Now then, Jimmy, now then. Don't you take any notice of him, miss. (*Slaps* JIMMY *on back.*) It's no more his fault than it's my fault or anybody else's fault. Here, you people—(*to the others*) we're not blaming Jimmy, are we?

OTHERS (*except* MISS TRANT *and* OAKROYD). No!

JOE. Who's been keeping our hearts up?

OTHERS. Jimmy!

JOE. Good old Jimmy!

OTHERS. Good old Jimmy!

OAKROYD (R., *rising*). Aye, that's right, good old Jimmy. (*Touches cap and sits again* R.)

MISS TRANT. I'm sure they're right. You're not to blame. None of you are. Only what are you going to do now?

NUNN. That's what we all want to know.

JOE. Haven't the faintest idea!

MRS. JOE. Not a glimmer! Gloom! Gloom!

(*Enter* MRS. MAUNDERS, C. *on stage—a fierce-looking elderly woman with a heavy grey fringe. She wears clothes and a hat of antiquated fashion and carries a large shopping-bag with vegetables in it.)*

MRS. MAUNDERS (C.). Do any of you actor-people know where Miss Longstaff is ?

ELSIE (*in a whisper to* MITCHAM). Keep in front of me, for the love o' mike. (*Gets behind* MITCHAM *to* L. *of him.*)

MRS. MAUNDERS. No use hiding, miss. (C.) I thought I'd catch yer here. Don't you try any o' your tricks on me. I've found your empty box in your bedroom.

ELSIE (*crosses to her,* L.C.). Comes o' poking your nose into other people's belongings, Mrs. Maunders.

MRS. MAUNDERS. None o' your sauce, *if* you please. I'll 'ave the police after you for trying to do a poor woman out of 'er rent. One pound three and sevenpence you owes me—includin' the washing.

ELSIE. I told you I'd written to my sister to help me out. Here's the pound. (*Takes note from her bag.*) This lady only just brought it this minute. (*Pointing to* MISS TRANT.)

MRS. MAUNDERS (*takes note and puts it in her purse*). Very like. Very like. And what about the other three and sevenpence ?

ELSIE. I'm afraid you'll have to wait for that.

MRS. MAUNDERS. I'm *not* going to wait.

(NUNN *rises.*)

You're going to pay me before you leave Rawsley or I'll 'ave the police after you.

NUNN. You wouldn't do that, Mrs. Maunders.

MRS. MAUNDERS. Wouldn't I ? Wouldn't I ?

MRS. JOE (*puts down her wool on basket and crosses to* MRS. MAUNDERS). For shame ! Have you no heart at all, woman ?

MRS. MAUNDERS. I'll woman you and your lot !

(MISS TRANT *rises.*)

Woman indeed ! What next ? Woman !

(JOE *rushes up steps,* L. *on to stage, to* MRS. JOE *and passes her in front of him to* L. JERRY, SUSIE, INIGO *return from* R. *on stage.*)

(*To* ELSIE.) You'll pay me here and now or I'll go straight off to the police. And we'll see then who's a woman.

(MITCHAM *goes behind basket,* L.C.)

MISS TRANT. This is too absurd ! (*Comes up steps* L. *on to stage* L.C. *To* MRS. MAUNDERS.) What did you say this young lady owed you ?

MRS. MAUNDERS (R.C.). Three and sevenpence.

MISS TRANT (L.C.). Three shillings and sevenpence ? (*Opens note-case.*)

MRS. MAUNDERS. You 'eard what I said.

MISS TRANT (*opening her bag*). There you are! A ten-shilling note.

(*She hands it across* ELSIE *to* MRS. MAUNDERS, *who drops it on the floor.*)

ELSIE (C.). Oh, you *are* kind, Miss Trant.
MISS TRANT. Sh! Sh!

(*See Plan 7.*)

MRS. MAUNDERS (*picking it up*). I haven't got any change.
MISS TRANT. Then get it at once. And see you give a receipt to Miss Longstaff as well.
MRS. MAUNDERS. I'm not in the 'abit o' giving receipts to my lodgers.
MISS TRANT. Well, you're going to in this case. And don't stand there and argue. Miss Longstaff, perhaps you'll go with this woman and settle the matter outside and bring me the change.
ELSIE. I will with pleasure. And what's more, too, I'll get back my box. Come on, Ma darling.

(*She goes off* C. *door, followed by* MRS. MAUNDERS, *who mutters under her breath.*)

(JERRY *goes* R. *and leans on props.*)

SUSIE (*going* R.C.). What did I say about the Fairy Queen? Didn't I tell you?

(NUNN *goes up steps* L. *to* L. *of* MISS TRANT, *who is* C.)

NUNN. D'you know, miss. This is really awfully good of you.
MISS TRANT (C., *shyly*). Oh, don't let's talk about it, *please*. It's—it's just this life of yours. It's so very different from anything I've ever known. D'you know somehow I'd like to learn more about it.
NUNN (L.C.). Well—are you staying here, Miss Trant?
MISS TRANT. Yes. I thought of going to that hotel in the Market-place.
NUNN. You mean the " Royal Standard "?
INIGO (*coming forward to* R. *of* MISS TRANT). Couldn't we all meet there? (*Addressing the whole company.*) Wait a minute, everybody. Will you all come to supper with me at the " Royal Standard " at, say, eight o'clock to-night? Then we can talk properly. That's all right, isn't it? (*To* MISS TRANT.)
MISS TRANT. I'd love it.
INIGO. Eight o'clock then, everybody.
MRS. JOE (*crossing to* INIGO). Very pleased indeed, I'm sure. With many thanks. (*Turns to* JOE, *then makes for door* C.) Joe—the props?

(MISS TRANT, SUSIE *and* INIGO *go down steps* R.)

Nunn. Yes, let's get these things down to the dressing-rooms.

(Nunn *gets hold of basket handle and* Mitcham *takes hold of other handle.*)

Joe. Half a mo'. I'll drop these curtains first. I promised the doorkeeper we would before we left the hall.

Mitcham. This reminds me—the time we played Rangoon during the earthquake our baggage——

(*The tabs fall as* Nunn *and* Mitcham *cross to* R. *with basket.*)

Oakroyd (C., *wistfully to* Miss Trant, *who has come* L.C.). Well, miss, I'd better 'ave them traps o' mine out o' t' car and be getting on like.

Miss Trant (L.C.). Oh, Mr. Oakroyd, where are you going?

Oakroyd. Nay, I don't know fairly.

Susie (*by piano,* R.). But he must come to supper too, mustn't he, Mr. Jollifant?

Inigo (*coming to* Oakroyd, R.C.). I said *everybody*, didn't I?—Of course he's included.

Miss Trant. Come along then, Mr. Oakroyd.

(*Moves towards the door and exits* L.)

Oakroyd (*to* Susie *and* Inigo *as he follows on to* L.C.). Well, this is a do, this is. This caps t' lot, this does.

Susie (R.). Tha's reight. Tha's said it t' first time.

Oakroyd (*to* Inigo). Yond's a caution. Her and our Lily's as like as two peas.

(*Exit* L.)

(Inigo *is about to follow when* Susie *runs to* R. *of him.*)

Susie. Just a minute, Mr. Inigo Jollifant! I've something to say to you.

Inigo. Good! (*Comes back* L.C.)

Susie (*comes to him,* C.). You see, it's awfully nice of you and all that, to invite us to supper. But you know, it isn't done, it really isn't done.

Inigo. What isn't done?

Susie. To ask a whole Company to supper like this. I mean, a manager might do it, or someone who's backing the show. But for anybody like you—a mere beginner, an amateur—it's not the thing.

Inigo. But they all accepted.

Susie (*laughs*). Yes, of course. But you be careful, young man, or they won't take you seriously. (*Turns away to* R.) And I must say I'd hate them not to take you seriously—

(Inigo *comes to her.*)

—with all the talent you've got.

INIGO. Oh, hang the talent! (*Turns away,* L.)

SUSIE (*turns up to him*). Now, don't you despise your talent. Just have a look at this paper. (*She crosses him and picks up "The Stage" from end chair.*) Look at the money the composer of the latest song-hit has made! Thousands! (*She forces the paper on him.*)

INIGO (*cross to* C.). Oh, I don't care about the money. I want my songs to be sung by *you.* That's all I want.

SUSIE (L.C.). You mean that I can have those songs of yours?

INIGO. Yes, and dozens more if you want 'em.

SUSIE. You're rather a darling, aren't you?

INIGO. Well, that's the point—am I? I mean, I wish you'd take *me* a bit more seriously—never mind the talent and the songs.

SUSIE. Oh—*you!* Who *are* you? (*Turns away to* L.)

INIGO. Who am I? I'm the chap who—well, you must have seen it from the start——

SUSIE (*with mock innocence*). Seen what, Mr. Jollifant?

INIGO. All the way here, I've been wanting to kiss you. I don't know why I didn't.

SUSIE. Oh, don't you? Well, I do. Because you've not been given a chance. (*Kneels on chair.*) Don't think I haven't seen that famous look in your eye—that fishy gleam.

(INIGO *sits* C.)

But—well, (*turns to him*) as they say in the book of words—you see before you a girl who is wedded to her art. And even if you're not wedded to *your* art, you might try a honeymoon with it.

INIGO (*rising and going to her*). Oh, but look here——

SUSIE (*sweetly*). Now let's talk about something else, shall we?

INIGO. There's nothing else in the world to talk about—nothing —absolutely. (*Puts hands on her arms as though to embrace her.*)

SUSIE (*sweetly*). Oh, isn't there?

(ELSIE *re-enters by the door* L. *below and coughs.* INIGO *turns away in disgust and sits* R.C.)

ELSIE. Beg pardon, but could you tell me where Miss Trant's gone? (*Stands by steps* L.)

SUSIE (L.C.). She's gone across to the "Royal Standard."

ELSIE. There now! And I've got her change. Took me all this time to settle with that Maunders female. Such a tongue! Called me everything in the farmyard. But I'm interrupting——

SUSIE. Of course you're not.

INIGO (*seated* R.C., *tersely*). Oh, not at all. (*He starts reading the paper.*)

ELSIE. Because if I am, do say so. I'd hate to be a spoil-sport. We've all got to have a bit of fun, haven't we? We're a long time dead, I always say.

SUSIE. Well, you can set your mind at rest as far as Mr. Jollifant and I are concerned. It's just artist to artist between us. Isn't that so, Mr. Jollifant ? (*Looks into his face teasingly.*)

INIGO (*reading furiously*). Oh, quite ! Quite ! Absolutely !

ELSIE. Well, personally, I know this much. If the right man came along I shouldn't hesitate to give my career the go-by. Believe me !

SUSIE (*icily*). Really ? How interesting—(*to* INIGO) I think I hear my uncle calling. See you later.

(*She goes off* L.)

(INIGO *takes a step as if to follow* SUSIE. ELSIE *puts up her finger which stops him. He turns and goes* c. *and sits and reads paper.*)

ELSIE (*realizing he is in love with* SUSIE). Poor boy !

(*She goes off by the lower door* L.)

(INIGO *in a rage tears the paper to pieces.*)

BLACK OUT.

SCENE 8

SCENE.—*Dining-room of the " Royal Standard," Rawsley.*

TIME.—*Evening.*

A typical large coffee-room of an old-fashioned country hotel. A big sideboard, very large engravings on the walls, etc. There is a dining-table in the c., *round which the Company is seated, and a piano on the* R. *An elderly* WAITER *has just served port.*
   (*See Photograph of Scene. Large set.*)

When the CURTAIN *rises the Company has just finished supper. They are drinking port. The* WAITER *wipes neck of bottle and puts it on sideboard.* NUNN *is discovered rising to the applause of the rest of the Company.*
   (*See Plan 8 for positions at table.*)

NUNN (*rising*). Ladies and gentlemen——
JOE. And not so much of the " ladies and gentlemen "——
MRS. JOE. Don't be vulgar, Joe.
NUNN. Well, boys and girls—I'm not going to say much. You've had a good dinner ; though as far as I'm concerned, there hasn't been a dinner. You ought to do the talking, not me. I only want to say that Miss Trant here, as you have guessed by this time, has decided to run the show.

(*Applause.*)

MISS TRANT. It was that horrid woman this afternoon. That

Mrs. Maunders that suddenly decided me to run this troupe. That's what did it!

(Applause.)

NUNN. Now I'm going to betray a secret. Something Miss Trant's confided to me that I think you ought to know. She's financing us to get us out of this mess, but don't think that means for a minute that she's a millionairess.

MISS TRANT (*laughingly*). Far from it—alas!

NUNN. All the more reason, if I may say so, that we should be grateful to you and work like blacks to make the show a success.

(Applause.)

In fact, we're going to turn it into the best little Concert Party on the road to-day.

(Applause.)

You'll be glad to know we're completing the Company at once. First by our old, or rather *young* friend, Miss Susie Dean, and if there's a better comedienne in Concert Party work to-day, I'd like to know who she is.

(Applause.)

Then again, Mr. Morton Mitcham is joining us.

(MITCHAM *rises.*)

Mr. Mitcham is not only Susie's uncle, but an artiste of great talent and long and wide and—er—thick—experience.

MITCHAM. Four times round the world. (*Sits.*)

(All laugh.)

(WAITER *exits* C.)

NUNN. As he says, four times round the world—Europe, Asia, Africa, America, Australia, and the Isle of Man. Am I right, sir? And then—in the place of the late pianist—Miss Maidstone—we have our friend Mr. Inigo Jollifant. He's new to the profession but he's a first-class pianist.

MRS. JOE (*gloomily*). Is he? I wonder.

NUNN. I ask you to remember too, boys and girls, that this is Mr. Jollifant's dinner.

(WAITER *re-enters* C. *and comes down to* R. *of* NUNN.)

MITCHAM. A feast! A feast!

(Applause.)

WAITER. Beg pardon, sir. Mrs. Tidby—that's the proprietor—sends 'er compliments and wishes to point out that it's long after closing time.

MITCHAM (*turns to* WAITER). And what of that, my good man ?

WAITER (*to* MITCHAM). Well, sir, some of our commercials have gone to bed and are complaining of the noise. Rawsley's an early town, sir, very early, if I may say so.

MITCHAM. You may *not* say so. Shall I not take mine ease at mine inn ?

(WAITER *scratches his head.*)

WAITER. Well, sir, Mrs. Tidby says she'll give you another ten minutes, but after that she's afraid she'll have to turn off the lights.

MITCHAM. Turn off the lights !—Let her dare ! Proceed, Mr. Nunn. Pay no attention to the scullion. Avaunt ! Avaunt !

(WAITER *does not comprehend.*)

NUNN. 'Op it !

(*The* WAITER *understands and retires. Exits* C. *hurriedly and off to* R.)

To resume. I've talked over the money side of the question with Miss Trant, and you'll hear all about that afterwards. First thing, then—rehearsals.

(*All groan.*)

We stop here and rehearse, this week.

(*Groans.*)

I know you don't like Rawsley. Another thing. Miss Trant does not like the *name* we've had for the show, and anyhow we ought to start afresh with another one—change the luck, y' know. So any ideas for a new name ?

JOE. Well, Jimmy, what about The Mugs ?

MRS. JOE. Don't be silly, Joe. The Mugs, indeed !

JOE. Well, that's an idea, isn't it ? Better than nothing.

MITCHAM. When I was up at Bangalore in nought-five, I coached a troupe there—professionally, you know—and they called themselves the Wallahs. What about reviving that ? The Wallahs ?

ELSIE. Putrid ! The Wallahs !

MITCHAM. Please yourselves. I only offer it as a suggestion. No doubt I shall think of something better in a moment.

MRS. JOE. I hope so !

MITCHAM. And while we're cudgelling our brains for a name for the show, I should like to say a few words. (*Rises.*)

(*Applause.*)

Now, ladies and gentlemen, friends and fellow artistes—

(ELSIE *giggles.*)

—I should like to propose—as I have proposed on many similar occasions in many different parts of the world—that we should display our grateful thanks to our host, your new colleague, and my friend—Mr. Inigo Jollifant!

(Applause.)

Mr. Jollifant and I have already had some extraordinary experiences together. We have gone through bad times and good times, and I have no doubt we shall go through many more still more extraordinary experiences and have many more good times—and bad times.

*(*MRS. JOE *takes glass from* ELSIE.*)*

I may say I saw at once when I first met him that he was a good trouper. And such he has proved himself to be to-night.

(Applause.)

And I propose that we all now raise our glasses—

*(*ELSIE *takes glass back.*)*

—and show our appreciation. Mr. Jollifant!

(All rise and his health is drunk, amid applause. Cries of " Speech."
All sit again.)

INIGO *(rising).* Well, ladies and gentlemen, I'm absolutely what-is-it—overwhelmed. I'm not very sure what a trouper is, but I'm jolly glad to know that I'm a good one. If it means being a good companion, then I'm proud to be called one—absolutely. Some-how—

*(*MISS TRANT *starts.)*

—there isn't too much—er—good companionship left in this world, is there? I mean, people don't seem to pull together much now, do they? Everybody—well, not everybody, but a lot of people—are out for a good time—and that's all right, of course. I'm all for it. The more the merrier, so to speak. But it's nearly always their own good time and nobody else's they're out after, isn't it?

(Various interjections from MITCHAM, JOE, *etc.)*

An awful lot of hard nuts about now, somehow—and only soft in the wrong places. Well, of course, I'm not better than anybody else, probably a bit worse——

MRS. JOE.   Oh! No!

INIGO.   But I'd like one or two people to say I was a good companion. That's where the fun comes in really, isn't it? I mean, a good crowd, all sticking together. Thanks very much. *(Suddenly sits down.)*

(Applause.)

MISS TRANT *(half rising).* Listen, everybody. Mr. Jollifant has given me the name for the show. I'm sure it's never been used before. We'll call ourselves " The Good Companions." What do you think of that ?   " The Good Companions."

INIGO. Jolly good.

(MISS TRANT *sits down again.*)

SUSIE. I like it. It's original. I don't know how it'll look on the bills though.

MRS. JOE (*in a deep and gloomy voice*). I do. It will look rotten on the bills.

ELSIE. Not enough dash about it.

JERRY. Too haybrow, Miss Trant.

NUNN. It's a bit on the stiff side and it won't space well on the bills—but it's out of the common.

MITCHAM. Just what I was going to say, Nunn—the very words.

MISS TRANT (*rises*). There it is, then ; we'll call ourselves—" The Good Companions." (*Sits.*)

(*General murmur.*)

OAKROYD (*rising and taking one step to* L.). Well, I'm nobbut one o' t' audience as you might say. But this is my bit. May you make good companions o' t' folk as comes to see and hear you, and nivver look back. (*Drinks.*)

MISS TRANT. Thank you, Mr. Oakroyd.

OAKROYD. Nay, you're welcome, miss. (*Pushes his chair in under table.*) And now it's about time for me to be sayin' good-bye and thank you. I'm i' t' road here. You can't do wi' me.

MISS TRANT. Just a minute, Mr. Oakroyd. Mr. Nunn here says that a handy man like you would be very useful to us.

NUNN. Stage carpenter, props and baggage man, curtain and lights, doorman when needed, bill-poster when needed. And of course any odd jobs.

OAKROYD (*standing* R.C.). Any odd jobs. Aye ! Just to fill in like.

SUSIE (*laughing*). Scored that time, Jess !

OAKROYD. Well, I know nowt about the-ayters. But I could pick a deal up, I daresay. Is it summat you want doing, or a reg'lar job ?

MISS TRANT. We want you to travel round with us, Mr. Oakroyd.

NUNN. Be part of the Company, of course. Wages three pounds ten a week, plus fares and extras.

OAKROYD. One o' t'—one o' " T " Good Companions," eh ? Well, by gow, I'll have a do at it. (*Pulling out his chair.*) I nivver thought I'd finish up as a the-ayter chap. (*Sits.*) This beats t' band, this does. (*Chuckles as he sits down.*)

MISS TRANT. That's all right, then. Will you come down to the Assembly Rooms in the morning ?

OAKROYD. At half-past six, wi' my tools.

MITCHAM (*holding his forehead*). Half-past six. My boy, there is no such time.

JOE. Half-past ten's the regular time.

OAKROYD. Day's half ower i' Bruddersford by then.

MITCHAM. Bruddersford? Did you say Bruddersford?

OAKROYD. Aye, Bruddersford! Happen you know it, Mr. Mitcham?

MITCHAM. I should think I did know Bruddersford. It's known in the profession as the comedian's grave.

OAKROYD. Eh, whativver for? (*Very solemn.*) They do say as a Bruddersford man is a good judge of a bad joke.

(JOLLIFANT *and* JOE *laugh*.)

MITCHAM (*taps on his glass, rising*). My friends, I give you "The Good Companions." Long life and good luck to 'em.

(*They all rise, raise their glasses. Only* MRS. JOE *does not get up.*)

NUNN. I'll drink this if it kills me.

MRS. JOE (*rising suddenly, slightly flushed*). One moment! Let me warn you! It's a grave mistake to drink to success beforehand! A grave mistake! It means nothing but disaster!

(*They sit again, except* MITCHAM *and* MRS. JOE.)

JOE. Oh, you and your superstitions.

MRS. JOE. I know! I can foresee—tragedy! (*Sits.*)

MITCHAM. Don't be ridiculous, Mrs. Joe. I foresee nothing but a rosy future, thanks to Miss Trant. I therefore reiterate—" The Good Companions."

(*All stand except* MRS. JOE. *All repeat* "The Good Companions," *but* MRS. JOE *shakes her head tragically.*)

INIGO (*drawing close to* SUSIE *and trying to embrace her*). "The Good Companions."

SUSIE. Here! None of that; put it into music. (*She pushes him over to the piano* R.)

(INIGO *begins playing* "Slippin' Round the Corner." ELSIE *and* JERRY *begin to dance.* MITCHAM, *who has produced his banjo, joins in the music.* MRS. JOE *dances with her husband.* SUSIE *starts dancing with* NUNN *and dances towards the side where* OAKROYD *is standing.*)

(*Turning to* OAKROYD *in imitation Yorkshire dialect, but still dancing with* NUNN). Now, lad! What about it? Coom on.

OAKROYD. All right, lass! We'll show 'em what we can do.

(SUSIE *leaves* NUNN *and dances with* OAKROYD. *The music quickens. All the couples dance with the exception of* NUNN, *who conducts the music on a chair with a big spoon, back of table* C. MISS TRANT *watches them all, very much interested and amused. Suddenly the*

D

lights go out. Only the hall beyond the archway is dimly lighted. The foreground is completely in the dark.)

WAITER (*in the archway*). Time, please, ladies and gentlemen. Time, please !

MITCHAM. She's turned out the lights.

JOE. The dirty old cat !

MRS. JOE. Joe ! No vulgarities !

ELSIE. Do remember the ladies. *Please !*

MISS TRANT. Well, I suppose we'd better be going.

(The following dialogue is practically spoken together, as the various characters find their way to the hall.)

NUNN. This way, Miss Trant—if you'll allow me to lead you——
(Exit, c.)

MISS TRANT. Oh, thank you. How very kind of you, Mr. Nunn.
(Exit, c.)

MRS. JOE. It's an insult to one's dignity ! An outrage !
(Exit. c.)

JOE. Now don't take on, old girl—steady ! Steady !
(Exit, c.)

ELSIE. Now, Jerry Jerningham ! None of your familiarities !
(Exit, c.)

JERRY. I'm nowhere near you. The idea !
(Exit, c.)

MITCHAM. The absurdity of this paternal government of ours. When I think of the night life of the Continent—not to mention India or China !

(Exit, c. OAKROYD exits c. They have all gone off except INIGO and SUSIE.)

INIGO (c. *in archway, in a half-whisper*). Susie ! Susie !
(Hall-light goes out.)

(SUSIE's laugh is heard as if still in the room.)

Susie ! I say, Susie ! Susie !
(The laugh is heard.)

Where are you ?—You little devil !

(Laugh from SUSIE. He knocks over a chair. There is a crash of china.)

Oh, hell !

CURTAIN.

ACT II

Scene 9

Scene.—*Lounge Bar of the Crown Hotel, Gatford.*

Time.—*Morning.*

*In the front of the stage is a lounge with easy chairs and a small table.
At the back* R. *is a bar. Back* C. *a door leads to the street.* L. *the
last steps of the staircase leading to the first floor. An archway down*
R. *leading off to the other parts of the hotel.*
(See Photograph of Scene. Large set.)

At the rise of the CURTAIN, *towards the* L. *are grouped " The Good
Companions " (with the exception of* OAKROYD). *In their midst*
ELSIE *and a youngish man. They are all of them facing a photographer and reporter, two shabbyish middle-aged men who are standing
down* R. *with a camera. All the others are very smart. The front
row are kneeling.* JERRY JERNINGHAM *has turned himself out most
elaborately for the occasion.*
(See Plan 9 for positions.)

PHOTOGRAPHER *(fussing about).* Now I think that's all right.
Just a little to the right there, please. Some of you can look at
the 'appy pair, and some can look at the camera. Just look natural,
ladies and gentlemen. *(Peeps through lens.)* That's very nice, very
nice indeed. Now, my friend will fire the flash, so be ready for it
and don't jump. Now steady, steady——

(The REPORTER *fires the flashlight. There is an affected scream from*
ELSIE. *Some of the others begin to laugh. The group breaks up.)*

MITCHAM *(to* ELSIE). My dear Mrs. Dulver, for, alas, you are
Elsie no longer to us, I remember when I was photographed with
the Maharajah of Bramapoor——

*(*LANDLORD *comes down* R. *He has been leaning against the bar during
photograph.)*

LANDLORD. Car's at the door!
ELSIE (C.). I should love to hear all about it. But I have only
just time to change into my going-away frock before we catch the
train, haven't I, dear ? *(She turns to her husband.)*

MRS. JOE (R.C.). Good-bye, my dear. (*Shakes hands.*) You'll be forgetting your old professional friends, I know!

ELSIE. Never! Never, Mrs. Joe!—Where's my bag? (*To her husband.*) Have you got my bag?

(*Some of the others' crowd round her. They gradually move up and off through the door.*)

(NUNN *appears from door* R. *with two soup plates full of dry rice.*)

NUNN (*crosses to* L.C.). Rice! Rice! Anybody want any *nice rice?*

(*All the following talk overlaps.*)

SUSIE. For the love of Mike don't step all over my new shoes!

MISS TRANT (C.). I do wish you all the happiness in the world, my dear.

JOE (R.C.). I think we ought to sing something. For she's a jolly good fellow, or something of the sort!

SUSIE. Why not many happy returns of the day?

(*The guests have all left, going off up stage* C.)

(JERRY *puts his tie straight at mirror* L., *then starts to go off down* R., *when* LADY PARTLIT *stops him.* LADY PARTLIT *comes down the stairs* L. *She is a handsome woman of thirty-eight, elaborately dressed with many jangling chains and jewels on her.*)

LADY PARTLIT (*as she comes downstairs to* JERRY, C.). Oh, just a moment!

JERRY (R.C., *turning*). Lady Partlit! What a serpraise!

LADY PARTLIT (C., *coquettishly*). Lady Partlit? Have you forgotten your promise?

JERRY. Prermise?

LADY PARTLIT. Yes. Didn't we agree yesterday that it was to be Dorothy and Jerry?

JERRY (*smiling at her*). Ser we did—Dorothay.

LADY PARTLIT. You got your cigarette-case?

JERRY. Loverlay! (*He takes it out of his pocket.*)

LADY PARTLIT. Did you like what I had put inside?

JERRY. Inserde? (*He opens it—he reads the inscription.*) Oh! Too divine!

(*He smiles at her. She smiles at him. They look about quickly. They see they are not observed. They kiss. Both giggle.*)

LADY PARTLIT. You're not rehearsing this afternoon?

JERRY. Not this afternoon. Ner.

LADY PARTLIT. Then why not come out in my car?

JERRY. Lerve to. (*Turns to go up* C.)

LADY PARTLIT. Not that way. I've left it waiting round the other side.

(*They go off by the archway* R. *almost running.*)

(*The* REPORTER *returns from the street with* NUNN *and* MITCHAM, C.)

REPORTER. Your Company's been a big success round here, hasn't it ? (*Coming down stage* R.C.)

NUNN (L.C.). A big success.

MITCHAM (C.). A riot, old man. An absolute riot.

REPORTER (*sitting* R.C., *making notes*). Good ! Now then, gentlemen, how long's the show been running ?

NUNN. Oh, about six months. Right through the winter.

MITCHAM. You can put that down, old man. Only Concert Party in England that's run right through the winter.

REPORTER. And where have you been ?

NUNN. Where haven't we been ?

MITCHAM. Five times round the world.

REPORTER (R.C.). What ?

MITCHAM (C.). Not this show. That's just me. Put that down, old man. Five times round the world.

NUNN (L.C.). Only five ? I thought it was six.

MITCHAM (C.). No, no. Don't let's exaggerate. Five times.

NUNN. That's right. We opened at Dotworth. Then we went to Sandybay.

MITCHAM. A tremendous success at the Pier Pavilion, Sandybay. Put that down, old man. Then we went to the Playhouse, Winstead——

NUNN. That's right. That's the place where I got this stuff—Pepsinate. That's the place. (*To* REPORTER—*crossing.*) I don't know if you suffer at all with your stomach—I'm fairly murdered with mine—but if you are, you try that Pepsinate. (*Producing bottle.*)

MITCHAM. Don't put that down, old man. What was next ? Haxby, that was it. The Kursaal, Haxby. Then Middleford. What came after Middleford ?

NUNN (C.). I can tell you that, all right. The old Theatre Royal, Towborough. They simply ate it there. Ate it !

MITCHAM (L.C.). All records broken in Luddenstall. Our light comedian and dancer—Jerry Jerningham—got twelve cigarette-cases on the last night. An absolute riot !

REPORTER. Good ! And what's the next move, gentlemen ?

NUNN. Well, we're considering an offer——

MITCHAM. A very big offer——

NUNN. For a residential season, right through the spring and summer, at one of our biggest seaside resorts.

MITCHAM. We're considering it. The offer's been made to us, and we're considering it. Put that down, old man.

REPORTER. I've got that. And what do you think of our local audiences ?

MITCHAM (*taking the stage*). In the course of a very long and varied experience——

NUNN. In all parts of the world——

MITCHAM (L.). I don't know that I've played to better audiences. Keen, generous, sympathetic, friendly.

NUNN (C.). Put *that* down, old man. (*To* REPORTER.)

REPORTER (*laughing*). Thanks very much. And if I want any other information, I shall know where to come. (*Rises and goes up* C.)

NUNN (R.C.). What about a quick one with us ?

REPORTER (C.). Thanks very much, but I won't. Matter of fact, I'm a teetotaller, gentlemen. Good morning, good morning.

(*Goes off quickly up stage* C. *to* R.)

MITCHAM (L.C.). A teetotaller ? And a newspaper man ? (*Shakes his head.*) Did you ever meet one before ?

NUNN. He can't have a regular job on the paper.

MITCHAM. Well, what about it ? (*Points to bar* R.)

NUNN. Just a tiddley.

(*They walk to the back of the bar to the* R. *and go out of sight.*)

(*Enter* RIDVERS *from street up* C. *as they disappear, and goes straight to the bar. He is a middle-aged man, gross, purple-faced, with a bowler hat at the back of his head and a large cigar in his mouth. He has an odd trick of sucking in his breath.*)

RIDVERS. Hello, hello ! (*Thumps bar counter.*) Come along, come along !

(LANDLORD *enters bar from* R.)

Oh, there you are, Tom. I didn't see you. Get me a double Scotch and a small soda.

LANDLORD (*serving him from behind bar*). Right you are, Mr. Ridvers. How's business, Mr. Ridvers ?

RIDVERS. Not too good.

LANDLORD. I should think these Good Companions have been knocking you a bit, haven't they, out at Stort and Mundley ? They say they're going to have a big week here at the Hippodrome. Two or three perhaps.

RIDVERS. Two or three nothing. We'll see about that.

LANDLORD. Oh ! They're a good turn.

RIDVERS. They're a damn' bad turn to me, Tom, I don't mind telling you.

LANDLORD. Why, I heard you were selling out your three picture palaces to a syndicate. Is that right ? A bit of competition won't matter much to you now.

RIDVERS. Oh, won't it ? That's all you know about it. Look here, my typist tells me that the woman who's running this pierrot show is staying here. Is that right ?

LANDLORD. ·That's right. Miss Trant, they call her.
RIDVERS. Well, I want to have a word with her. Is she in ?
LANDLORD. She was outside a minute ago, seeing the bride off.

(MISS TRANT *enters* C. *and goes up a few stairs* L.)

Here she is now. Miss Trant, this gentleman, Mr. Ridvers, wants
to speak to you a minute.

(*Indicates* RIDVERS, *who steps forward.*)

MISS TRANT. Who ? Oh, I see. (*She comes down and across to*
R.) Well, you can speak to me here.

(RIDVERS *comes down on her,* L.)

RIDVERS (*keeping his hat on and puffing out cigar smoke and coming
very close to* MISS TRANT, *who continually looks away from him*).
That's it. My name's Ridvers, and I don't mind telling you *I'm*
the Triangle New Era Cinema, *U*nlimited. I've got a picture house
in each of these three towns, Gatford, Stort and Mundley. Well
known here, *very* well known, *not* a stranger to the district.
MISS TRANT (*trying to dodge the smoke and looking at him with
dislike*). I'm afraid I don't understand.
RIDVERS. You're this Miss Trant who's running these what's
it—Companions' pierrot show, aren't you ?
MISS TRANT (R.). Yes. What do you want ? (*Looks pointedly
at his hat and cigar and backs away from him.*)
RIDVERS (R.C., *following her*). Doing damned well here, aren't
you ?
MISS TRANT (R., *annoyed*). I beg your pardon !
RIDVERS (R.C.). Not at all ! Not at all ! Doing damned well
here, aren't you ? (*Flicks cigar-ash between them, and then points
cigar at her.*) And do you know at whose *expense* you're doing so
damned well ? At *mine*. At *my* expense. And I'm here to have
a little talk about it.
MISS TRANT (*furious*). I don't want to have a talk about it.
(*She tries to cross to stairs.*)
RIDVERS. Perhaps not, but I do. (*Stands in front of her, barring
the way.*)
MISS TRANT. Will you please get out of the way at once. I don't
want to talk to you about anything.
RIDVERS. What's the idea ? Going on like this ? (*Does not
move.*)
MISS TRANT. Please get out of the way. If you don't I'll **ask**
the manager to put you out.

(RIDVERS *reluctantly makes way.* MITCHAM *and* NUNN *come from
behind bar* R.)

(MISS TRANT *sweeps past him and goes out rapidly upstairs.*)

RIDVERS (*staring after her*). Well, my God! (*Goes to bar* R.C.) Let's have another double, Tom. That's a swine of a woman you've got there.

MITCHAM (C.). Let me tell you, sir, that's no way to talk about a lady.

NUNN (L.C.). That is so. Just keep your swine to yourself.

RIDVERS. Who the hell are you? (*Turns on them.*)

LANDLORD. These two gentlemen are members of the troupe.

RIDVERS. Ah! Ah! So this is what they're all paying their money to see, is it, Tom? Broken-down old pros. Buskers.

NUNN. You want a good mouthwash.

(RIDVERS *turns on him.*)

LANDLORD. Now then, gents, let's all be friendly. This is Mr. Ridvers who runs the cinemas round here.

MITCHAM (*looking at* NUNN). Ah! Ah!

NUNN (C., *returning glance*). Ah! Ah!

RIDVERS (R.C., *truculently*). What you ah-ahing about?

MITCHAM (L.C.). Nunn, do you remember that dirty little place where we threw ninepence away the other afternoon?

NUNN (C.). And we wondered how people could pay money to go in. Is that the place?

(RIDVERS *angrily makes right for them.* NUNN *jumps round behind* MITCHAM.)

RIDVERS (R.C.). You're both very funny, aren't you? Couple o' buskers. Going round with the hat. Dirty pierrots, the pair of you.

(*They back away from him.*)

LANDLORD (R.). Easy, Mr. Ridvers, easy.

MITCHAM (C.). I've been in places where you'd have had a bullet through you—zip—like that—for saying less than you've said about a lady.

(JOE *enters at the back* R. *and comes slowly behind* RIDVERS *to his* R.)

RIDVERS (C., *fiercely, threatening them*). Go and have a look at yourselves. I'll say what I like and you won't stop me, and you know you won't. D'you see? I'll say what I like.

(*They back a step.*)

JOE (R.C.). Oh, you will, will you? (*Examines him curiously.*)

RIDVERS (*turns hurriedly to* JOE). What? (*Standing his ground.*) Well, what's wrong with me?

JOE (*menacingly*). I'll tell you what isn't wrong with me! I'm a pierrot, same as these two. A dirty little pierrot. A broken-down pro. A busker. Just the same.

(*Louder now, with* RIDVERS *retreating.* MITCHAM *and* NUNN *retreat behind them to table down* R.)

Now I'll tell you what's the matter with *you.* You've two names. You have two names. One's Mud and the other's Walker. Now get outside. Quick! Outside! You've just time. Oh! (*Following him.*) You're just the right shape and size, you are.—I couldn't half give you a slugging.

(RIDVERS *disappears through door* C. *And then* JOE *retreats backwards towards the* L. *with* MRS. JOE *pursuing him.*)

MRS. JOE (C.). Slugging indeed! Isn't that a nice way to talk, and in a public place too. I'm ashamed of you, Joe Brundit, I really am.

JOE (L.). All right, old girl. Sorry.

MRS. JOE. Sorry indeed! You make me blush!

JOE. All right, ease up a bit. He was throwing his insults about, that chap, calling Miss Trant all the names under the sun.

MRS. JOE. He'd better not let me hear him. I saw the sort of man he was in a minute. And who's *he* to start calling her names?

JOE. He was calling us all dirty little pierrots, buskers, broken-down old pros, and all the rest of it.

(MITCHAM *stands by table* R. NUNN *sits in chair* R. *of table* R.)

MRS. JOE. Oh, he was, was he? Well, what do you want to stand here for, a man of your size, Joe, letting him call you anything he fancied?

(SUSIE *and* INIGO *enter* C.)

Haven't you any spirit at all? My word, if I'd heard him. (*Crosses to chair* R.C.)

JOE. Well, I'll be blowed. (*Crosses to* MITCHAM, *to* NUNN, *etc.*) Did you hear that? And just this minute she was blaming me——

INIGO (*coming down* C.). Has Miss Trant made up her mind about that Bournemouth offer?

(SUSIE *goes over and sits in wicker chair* L., *looking despondent.*)

MRS. JOE. Ah! I've been waiting for something definite about the Bournemouth offer. When I heard of it, I said to Joe at once, " The luck has completely changed. We're made. A big town," I told him, " a town with Tone and Taste."

MITCHAM (*behind table, leaning against bar* R. *with* JOE). You've said it. Tone and Taste—and money.

MRS. JOE. Five months at least guaranteed—it's a miracle. If you'd gone round the coast and told me you were trying to find a place for a residential season, I should have told you without the slightest hesitation—Bournemouth by all means. And Bournemouth now it is. But nothing so far seems to have been done about it, nothing.

NUNN (*seated* R.). Well, you see, it's like this——

MRS. JOE. I hope there's no haggling about terms. Surely Bournemouth wouldn't haggle.

SUSIE (L.). Oh, don't worry about it, Mrs. Joe.

MRS. JOE. I'm not worrying, my dear. I merely want to know. You don't, because you don't care. Admit it.

SUSIE (*rising and coming* C. *and wildly facing them all*). All right, I will admit it. You're all beginning to wonder what's the matter with me and telling me I'm restless. Well, I'll tell you the truth. I suppose I'm always thinking something absolutely marvellous is going to turn up, and then when you all come along and say, "Hurray! Six months in Bournemouth! Susie will continue to sing number twenty-seven on the programme. Twice daily!" Well, then I see the same old stick-in-the-mud business going on and on, and I think—"Oh hell!"

MRS. JOE (*reproachfully*). Not hell, my dear, not hell!

SUSIE. Yes—hell! I just see myself stuck there, and other girls I know are getting West End parts. With those numbers of Inigo's —I could go anywhere—anywhere! Oh—sorry! (*Turns* L.C.) I'm a fool, I suppose. (*Goes* L.)

(*She sits* L. *and breaks down, and is comforted by* INIGO, *who crosses and stands at back of chair* L.)

NUNN (*crossing to* R. *of* SUSIE). Just a minute, Susie. We can't do much for you, my dear, but we can try.

(INIGO *closes the curtains.*)

Now watch me, Susie!

(*He takes a folded poster out of his pocket, and goes through* C. *of curtains, then reappears holding out the poster, imitating a trumpet. He unrolls the poster and shows it to* SUSIE. *The poster—a double-crown—says:* "*Gatford Hippodrome. The Good Companions. Birthday Benefit for Susie Dean, The Darling of Gatford. Book Now! Book Now! Book Now!*"

(C.). Ta-ra!

SUSIE (*thrilled—getting up from chair*). You're giving me a benefit!

MRS. JOE (R.C.). Well, we knew it was your birthday, Susie, on Saturday. And we thought this would be a nice little surprise.

SUSIE (*coming* C.). It is, it's the loveliest surprise. It was sweet of you all. And you must think I'm an ungrateful little rotter. (*She recovers completely.*)

JOE. We don't.

SUSIE. Well, I've got a surprise, too. Not much of a one, but I decided this morning to give a birthday tea-party after the Matinée on Saturday. And I count on you all coming. Details to follow.

(*She takes out her vanity-bag and powder and makes up her face, going down* L.C.)

JOE. We'll be there, Susie. And now what about a little lunch to follow? (*To* MRS. JOE.) What's it going to be to-day, Missus?

NUNN (C., *facetiously*). The hind-quarters of yesterday's rabbit.

MRS. JOE (*majestically*). Boiled beef and carrots.

(*She sweeps off by the archway down* R. *with* JOE.)

MITCHAM (*with a gesture of invitation, turning to* SUSIE). Susie, my child——

(*At a look from* INIGO *he turns to* NUNN *and lays his hand on the other man's shoulder.*)

Nay, come! Let's go together!

(MITCHAM *and* NUNN *go off down* R.)

INIGO (L., *speaking to* SUSIE *with sudden decision*). I should like to talk to you.

SUSIE (R.C., *wide-eyed, turning to him*). Yes?

INIGO (*solemnly*). To have it out with you just for once!

SUSIE (C., *mock-heroically*). "To have it out just for once!"

INIGO. Why do you keep on guying me, Susie? You've been unbearable lately, absolutely. And you know what I feel and think about you. (*Crosses to* L.C.)

SUSIE (*turning, very sweetly*). No, I don't. Tell me.

INIGO. I think you're . . . (*He can't go on, but just gives a groan and crosses* L. *to desk.*) What's the use? It's all just fun for you, Susie. You don't really care a damn.

SUSIE. Why don't you go on to the next part, Inigo?

INIGO. What's that?

SUSIE. You ought to say now, "If you think I'm the kind of man you can play with, you're wrong."

INIGO. I suppose you're sick of seeing me about. But I wouldn't be here at all if it weren't for you. If *you* went, I wouldn't stick it out another week.

SUSIE. No, and I'll tell you why. It's all just fun for you, Inigo. You don't really care a damn.

INIGO. Oh, don't I?

SUSIE. No, you don't. This business—the stage—is just a game to you. Well, it isn't to *me*. I'm a pro. I belong to the theatre. I was nearly born in a dressing-room, and I hope I'll die in one. I'm not doing this for fun, young fellow. I want to get on. God! If I don't get on soon, I'll bust.

INIGO. What do you want me to do to help you?

SUSIE. You? I don't want you to help *me*. I can look after myself. But why don't *you* go and do something for yourself?

INIGO. For myself?

SUSIE. Yes, with those songs of yours. Look at that new number, "Slippin' Round the Corner." Don't you realize that Felder and Hunterman's are the best music publishers in London? And their traveller was crazy about your songs.

INIGO. Their traveller? Oh, you mean that fellow Milbrau. He came to see me, but I couldn't stand the sight of his teeth and pink shirt. He looked like a shark disguised as a salmon.

SUSIE. That's you all over. That's just the way you throw away your chances.

INIGO. Oh rot!

SUSIE. It's the way you hang about and don't do a *thing* that irritates me. You make me sick!

INIGO (*reproachfully*). Susie!

SUSIE. You're an amateur!

INIGO. Pooh!

SUSIE. And you're so—so—feeble.

INIGO. What?

SUSIE. I said feeble.

INIGO. Say it again.

SUSIE. All right. Feeble, feeble, feeble!

INIGO. So that's it, is it?

SUSIE. Yes. That's it.

(INIGO *hesitates a second, then goes suddenly to the writing-table, finds a telegram form in the drawer, sits down and writes out a telegram.*)

What are you doing, Inigo?

INIGO (*getting up, telegram in hand*). If you really want to know —I've just feebly written a feeble telegram.

SUSIE. What's in it?

INIGO. Wait and see.

SUSIE. I want to read it. I must.

(*She makes a dash for it and is caught by* INIGO *and soundly kissed.*)

INIGO. Feeble, am I? (*Waving the telegram.*) Good-bye.

(*He rushes off through the curtains.*)

SUSIE (*furiously*). Pig!——

(*When he has left—with a smile.*)

Darling!

BLACK OUT.

SCENE 10

SCENE.—MR. PITSNER'S *private office at Felder and Hunterman's, the music publishers.*

It is only a corner angle of the office, half a reception-room and quietly and nicely furnished. On the R. *a grand piano is seen.* C. *the door. On the wall* L. *a desk, and behind it a chair. Easy chair between the desk and the door.*

(*See Photograph of Scene. Small set.*)

At the desk sits Mr. Pitsner, *a thin, grey man, with a very tired,
melancholy manner.* Monte Mortimer, *a florid man of forty-
five, sits on the easy chair. His manner is most important and
majestic.* Ethel Georgia, *a gorgeous blonde musical comedy star,
is singing* c. *to* Inigo's *playing.*

Pitsner (*as* Inigo *finishes*). Well, my dear, what do you think
of that number ?

Ethel (R.C.). What do I think of that number ? (*Looking at*
Inigo.)

Pitsner. And the number before ? And the number before
that ? You haven't said a word yet.

Ethel (*still gazing at* Inigo). No. I know I haven't. But I'll
tell you now.

Monte (L.C.). Let me do the talking, my dear Ethel——

Ethel (*turning and going* c.). No, Mr. Monte Mortimer, I don't
care what you're going to say. I tell you, just as sure as my name's
Ethel Georgia, I mean to sing all three of those numbers in your
new revue. Take my word for that.

Monte (*evasively*). We'll see. We'll see about that.

Ethel. See nothing ! Mr. Pitsner, *you* think they're winners,
don't you ?

Monte. Of course he'd say so whether he thought so or not.
He's trying to sell them to me.

Pitsner (L.). I can sell them like hot cakes. Hot cakes !
Memsworth'll jump at 'em.

Monte (L.C.). Memsworth !

Pitsner. You don't want a rival manager like Memsworth to
get 'em. You're the first to hear them, Mr. Mortimer. Mr. Jollifant
only got to London two hours ago. And if I hadn't had Milbrau's
letter recommending him, I wouldn't have even received him. You
know what tripe most of these so-called song-writers turn out
nowadays !

Ethel. Well, this certainly isn't tripe ! (*Sits on arm of* Monte's
chair L.C.)

Pitsner. No. It certainly is *not*. It's everything that Milbrau
said it was. I've always maintained that Milbrau's the smartest
man that Felder and Hunterman have got on the road.

Ethel. And Felder and Hunterman are the smartest people in
the music-publishing business.

Pitsner. Just like you're the smartest revue artiste on the stage
to-day and Mr. Mortimer is the smartest showman in the London
entertainment world.

Inigo (*rising*). Just as I'm the smartest song-writer, I suppose.

Ethel (*rising and crossing to* c.). Well, you are ! No doubt of
that—isn't he, Monte ?

Monte (*vaguely*). Is he ?

Ethel (*going to* Monte, L.C.). Come on, Monte. Speak up.

I've got an appointment at the hairdresser's. I'm late already as it is! You'll get those numbers for me? That's settled?

MONTE. I'm not so sure about that, Ethel.

ETHEL. I am, Monte. I want them.

MONTE. We'll see about it. Run along to your hairdresser.

ETHEL (*twisting his hair on top*). I will, but if you don't get them for me, *you*'ll never want a hairdresser again. (*She slaps top of* MONTE's *head.*)

MONTE. I'll think it over.

ETHEL. It doesn't want any thinking. You can't let stuff like that go. Good Lord, you've only *got* one number in the show that's worth a *damn* so far. These are absolute winners.

MONTE. Run along, dear.

ETHEL. I'll run too far for you, if you don't do what I ask. Buy the bunch. And keep this boy busy. Good-bye, Mr. Jollifant. (*Goes to* INIGO *and shakes hands.*) And don't forget—I'll make your fortune for you. Good-bye, Mr. Pitsner. Monte, I expect you in my dressing-room to-night with those numbers in your hand! Be good, sweetheart. (*To* INIGO, *who opens door for her* C.) Au revoir!

(*She goes off* C.)

(*As she goes,* INIGO *wipes his brow with relief.*)

MONTE (*with a sigh*). Well—let's get to business. (L.C.) Supposing I did take these numbers of yours—what would you say?

INIGO (C.). Well—as a matter of fact, I've a good deal to say.

MONTE. I know. Terms, of course. Don't worry. The terms will be all right. They're going to surprise you.

INIGO. I've got some terms, too. I hope they won't surprise you. But they might.

PITSNER. I must say I don't quite understand this.

MONTE. What's the idea?

INIGO (*rather nervously, facing them*). It's like this. There's nothing very mysterious about it. You see there's a girl in this show of ours, and she's tremendously clever, she's absolutely marvellous—everybody who's seen her says so. She's our comedienne and her name's Susie Dean—and she hasn't had a decent chance yet. She's going to have one now.

MONTE. My dear chap——

INIGO. Just a minute, listen. We're giving a show to-night, at the Gatford Hippodrome. As a matter of fact it's her benefit. And if you really want these songs of mine, you've got to come down and see her.

MONTE (*rising and going* C.). What, *me*? Monte Mortimer? Go down to look at a girl in a Concert Party? My dear chap, it couldn't be done, couldn't possibly be done.

INIGO (*stubbornly*). Sorry. (*Crosses* R.)

MONTE (*following to* R.C.). I've got far too much to do. Far too much. Mind you, I don't say that if the girl came up to London sometime I'm not ready to give her an audition. Any time you like. And if she's all right, I'll give her some chorus work, or perhaps even a few lines to speak.

INIGO (R.C.). That's not the idea at all, Mr. Mortimer. I'm not trying to blackmail you into shoving her into the chorus. All I ask is that you should come down and see her to-night. If you see her working, you'll jump at her.

MONTE (*crossing to* L.C.). Oh! Pitsner, what shall I . . .

PITSNER. Mr. Jollifant, I don't think you realize what a chance you're throwing away yourself by talking like this. Just think of Ethel Georgia. What'll she say to it?

INIGO (R.C.). Sorry, Mr. Pitsner, but I honestly don't give a damn.

MONTE (*crossing to* C.). Look here, my dear chap, you're very clever and you're going a long way, but you don't know yet how these things are done.

INIGO. Listen, Mr. Mortimer. You never heard of these songs of mine before, did you? Well, this girl's better than these songs. Take my word for it. Why, if somebody had told you yesterday about these songs of mine, you wouldn't have believed *them.*

MONTE. But now I've heard the songs.

INIGO. Yes, and to-night you'll see the girl.

MONTE. To-night! You're crazy!

INIGO. The place is Gatford!

MONTE. I never heard of it. (*Moans comically.*) Gatford! Gatford! To-night at Gatford! (*Crosses to* L.C. *and back to* C.) Oh, come now, you've had your laugh—let's talk sense, let's get down to business.

INIGO. I've got down to it—I'm up to the neck in it—absolutely. *No Gatford, no songs.*

MONTE. You can't dictate to me like that. You're cutting your own throat.

INIGO. Well, whose throat do you want me to cut?

(MONTE *mops his brow.*)

I tell you, I don't give a damn. If that girl doesn't get her chance, I don't want mine. I'm serious. (*He rolls up his music and takes up his hat.*)

MONTE (*crosses to table* L.C. *After exchanging a few whispered remarks with* PITSNER, L.C.). All right, I'll go there. It wrecks the rest of this day, but I can fix that. (*Turns to* INIGO.) The Gatford Hippodrome? All right. You'll see me there. So long, Pitsner. I'll see you some time on Monday. (*Goes to door* C.)

INIGO. And I can count on your being there to-night?

MONTE. You can—blast you! So long!

(*Goes out* C.)

INIGO (*drawing long breath*). And that's that.

PITSNER. It is.

INIGO (*picking up hat, coat and music from piano*). I must go, too. But I should like to ask you a question, Mr. Pitsner. (*Goes L.C.*)

PITSNER. Yes ?

INIGO. You're a man of experience. Now do you honestly think I can be described as feeble ?

PITSNER. As what ?

INIGO. Feeble is the word.

PITSNER. Why do you ask ?

INIGO. Well, somebody I know told me I was feeble. What do *you* think ?

PITSNER (*sadly, solemnly*). I could call you many things. You're a young man who could be called many things. But not feeble, not feeble.

INIGO (*shaking hands violently*). Thanks very much. That's all I wanted to know. (*Rushes to door* C.)

PITSNER. And another thing.

INIGO (*stopping on way to door*). What's that ?

PITSNER. You can tell her I said so. (*Chuckles softly.*)

BLACK OUT.

SCENE 11

SCENE.—*Behind the scenes at the Gatford Hippodrome.*

TIME.—*Saturday night.*

In front is a switchboard, R.C. *There is plenty of room at the back, as the full stage entrance to and from the dressing-rooms is to the* L. *The men entering from the audience come in from the* R.
     (*See Photograph of Scene. Large set.*)

When the CURTAIN *rises, the Concert Party, all in some fancy Pierrot costume, can just be seen, and can be plainly heard singing the final chorus before the interval.*
     (*See Plan 10 for positions during final chorus.*)

OAKROYD *is standing in the near wing, by the switchboard* R., *ready to work the lights and attend to the Curtain.* MISS TRANT *comes round from the* L. *and stands near him, watching the stage. When the chorus is finished and the Curtain of the inner stage comes down, there is a great deal of applause but also some booing and cat-calls, obviously coming from the back of the auditorium. After two Curtains* OAKROYD *switches off footlights and battens, and comes down to* L. *of* MISS TRANT, *who is down* R.

OAKROYD. There's a whole lot on 'em at t' back o' t' pit makking all t' commotion. T' attendant there can do nowt wi' 'em. There's too monny of 'em an' he's too owd. He answers to sixty—and by gow !—by the look of him he might be eighty.

(MRS. JOE, JOE *and* NUNN *come off the stage down* L. *of* OAKROYD.)

MRS. JOE. You couldn't want a better audience if it wasn't for those people at the back.

JOE. I've a good mind to go round and have a look at some of those chaps.

MRS. JOE. You've a good mind to do nothing of the sort.

NUNN. No, leave 'em alone, Joe. If they start it in the second half, I'll make a speech from the stage about it.

(*They exit* L.)

MISS TRANT (R.). Can't he keep them quiet ?

(SUSIE *comes down* L. *of* OAKROYD.)

(*See Plan* 11.)

OAKROYD. Not he. I went round me-sen about half an hour sin, and I said to him, " You'd better fetch a bobby, mate, if you can't do no better nor this. There's going to be ructions here ! "

MISS TRANT (R.). Ructions ?

OAKROYD. Aye, ructions. Don't you know what them is, miss ? Well, it's what we're going to have here, if we don't keep our heads screwed on.

MISS TRANT (*crossing to* L.). If there's any more of it, I'm going to have them turned out. It's vile and unpardonable, and I'm not going to have it.

(*Exits* L.)

(OAKROYD *goes up stage and collects stools and takes them off up* L. MITCHAM *and* JERRY *come down and go off down* L. SUSIE *is going with them, when* INIGO *rushes after her, gets hold of her arm and detains her.*)

INIGO (R.C.). Susie, you must listen, you must. It's terribly important.

SUSIE (C., *stopping ; very coldly*). Well ?

INIGO. I'm awfully sorry I couldn't get back in time for your birthday party. I've gone and forgotten your present, too.

SUSIE (*coldly*). I thought you said it was important. Is that all ? (*Turning to go.*)

INIGO. No, there's a lot more.

SUSIE (*trying to get away*). I don't want to hear any more, thank you.

INIGO (*still holding her arm*). But you must listen, Susie.

SUSIE. Let me go.

INIGO. I won't until you've heard what I have to say. You see, I had to go up to London to-day—— (*Releases her arm.*)

E

Susie (*with marked change of tone and attitude and turning to him*). London !

Inigo. Yes, London. I didn't tell anybody I was going. I had to see Felder and Hunterman.

Susie (*eagerly*). Inigo ! Your songs ! They've been hearing them. Have they taken them ? Do tell me, quick.

Inigo (*slowly*). They want them all right. (*Turns away* R.)

Susie (*following to* C.). Oh, go on, go on. You're so *slow*. Tell me all about it quick. If you don't, I shall think you're feeble again.

Inigo (*turning to her*, R.C.). Well, you see, that man Monte Mortimer heard them too and——

Susie (L.C.). Inigo ! (*Then changing tone.*) You're pulling my leg. You never saw Monte Mortimer. (*Turns away* L.)

Inigo. I did, woman, I did. And what's more, he wants them for his new revue.

Susie (*coming back* C.). He doesn't !

Inigo. And you can see him, too. I'll show him to you, if you like.

Susie (*shaking him*). Inigo, don't be so daft ! (*Turns* L.C. *and back again.*) He's not here. He *can't* be here.

Inigo. He *is*, I tell you. In the stalls next to the aisle on the second row.

Susie. *The* Monte Mortimer. But what's he doing here ?

Inigo. I made him come here to see you. I said if he didn't, he couldn't have my songs.

Susie. Inigo, if you're being funny, I'll never speak to you again—never, never, never.

Inigo. My dear, I made him come and he's here. I saw him come in.

Susie (*wild with excitement*). You angel ! (*Embracing him.*) Show me. Where is he ?

(*They rush on to the stage, peep through the spyhole in Curtain*—Susie *talking wildly as she returns.* Inigo *comes down after her on her* L.)

Let me think a minute. No, I can't think. I'm all in bits. I shall make a mess of it now. I know I shall. (R.C.)

Inigo (C.). Perhaps I oughtn't to have told you.

Susie. Don't be ridiculous. Of course you ought. I'd never have forgiven you if you hadn't. I shall be all right when the time comes. If I'm not, then I'm no good. Gosh, what a chance ! Suppose he doesn't like me. Oh, I shall die if he doesn't.

Inigo (L.C.). He'll like you all right. If he doesn't he's a fat-head—absolutely. And he won't get any songs of mine. Under which king, Besonian, speak or die ! That's what I shall say to him. (*Strikes attitude.*)

Susie (c., *squeezing his arm*). Darling! But look here, Inigo, I won't have you tying those songs of yours to me like that.

Inigo. You can't stop me. I insist on tying them to you. I want to tie everything to you. I want to tie myself to you. (*Turns L.*) But I'm sorry I couldn't get back sooner for your party—and I forgot your present, too.

Susie. You didn't. The great Monte's my present. Marvellous present. The best I could have had.

Inigo. And I never wished you anything. It isn't too late, is it? Many happy returns of the day, Susie.

(Oakroyd *enters up* L. *and comes down* L.C.)

Susie. Thank you. (*Then whirls round.*) Oh—I'm an idiot— but I'm so happy. Inigo, you're a darling.

(*Flings her arms about him and kisses him, all in a flash.*)

Oh, my make-up!

(*Then hurries out down* L.)

Inigo (*drawing deep breath*). Ah! (*Throws his hat in the air and catches it.*)

Oakroyd (L.C.). What's up wi' Soosie? And what's up wi' you?

Inigo. I've just told her there's a big theatrical man from London come down to see her.

(Mrs. Joe *and* Nunn *run on from* L.)

Oakroyd. Champion! Hello, here's some more all of a dither (*He crosses behind to* R.)

Nunn (*going up to* Inigo, c.). I say, Monte Mortimer's not in front to-night, is he? I've heard those yarns before. He isn't, is he?

Inigo (R.C.). Yes, he is.

Mrs. Joe (L.C.). He's in the box, isn't he? As soon as I saw those people in evening dress in the box, I said to myself—" Now *somebody's* arrived."

(Nunn *goes up and looks through spyhole.*)

Inigo (R.C.). No, he's not in the box. He's in the stalls—second row—next to the aisle.

(Susie *enters down* L.)

Mrs. Joe. What a chance, oh, what a chance! I'm just saying, my dear—(*to* Susie) what a chance!

(*They go up stage, leaving* Susie *with* Oakroyd.)

Susie (c.). I know! *What* a chance! I'm nearly bursting. Jess, lad, I'm nearly bursting.

OAKROYD (R.C.). Aye, I've heard about it. Nar, steady, lass, steady on. Tak' it easy!

SUSIE. I can't. I'm too excited.

(Waltzes him round.)

OAKROYD (C.). And what about poor old Good Companions? If he gives you a job we'll nivver see you ner more, unless we go up on a day trip and pay to go in.

SUSIE (R.C.). Oh, don't say that, Jess. *(Takes hold of his arm.)*

OAKROYD. Never you mind, Soos lass, you look after yer-sen, and if yon feller does offer you ten pound a week to go up to London, tak' it on. So long as there's nowt shameless about it, coming on naked and suchlike.

SUSIE *(with mock modesty)*. Jess, lad. You've got a nasty mind. You might be a town councillor.

OAKROYD. Well, you'll ha' to mind that, I'm thinkin', for they're a bit of a foul lot i' London, they tell me. But if it's decent-like, tak' it. Aaaa, but I'd right miss you if you went, I should an' all——

SUSIE. Darling! *(Squeezing his arm.)* I think you're marvellous, Jess lad, and I'd miss you too. Let's run away to Canada together, shall we?

OAKROYD *(takes hold of her hands)*. Aaaa, there's nowt I'd like better. We *would* have a do—you and our Lily and me.

(OAKROYD goes to switchboard R.)

(SUSIE exits down L.)

(JOE and MITCHAM enter from the L.)

NUNN *(coming forward again)*. All right, Inigo. Where's Jerry? Never mind. Joe first—one number. And cut it short, Joe, if there's any trouble. Then Mrs. Joe. Right you are, Inigo.

(INIGO *goes up to piano. The Curtain rises. JOE goes on stage and announces his number. MITCHAM, MRS. JOE and NUNN are down stage R. OAKROYD is at switchboard. MISS TRANT enters down L. as number commences, and joins the others over R.)*

JOE *(on the inner stage)*. Ladies and gentlemen——
VOICE IN CROWD. Hullo!
JOE. —by special request—" The Trumpeter."
VOICE. What for?

(Applause from the audience, but a voice from the back, loud and clear, calls " Shirrup! " and there is some laughter and some " shushing." JOE sings, " Trumpeter, what are you sounding now? " Whistle off.)

JOE *(very angrily)*. If the gentleman at the back doesn't shut up, he'll soon be made to shut up.

NUNN (*whispering*). Steady, Joe boy, steady.

(*There is another uproar, a mixture of applause, " shushing," cries of " Turn him out " and derisive noises from the back. When this has subsided, JOE sings. Uproar starts quietly and continues through next few lines.*)

MRS. JOE (*talking through music*). Miss Trant, Jimmy, I'm convinced, I'm perfectly convinced, it's all a put-up affair.

NUNN (*gloomily*). Looks like it, doesn't it ?

MISS TRANT. Do you really think so ? Surely it can't be.

MRS. JOE. I've had my suspicions for some time. Now I'm convinced.

MISS TRANT. I'm going through the pass-door to see if anything can be done about it.

(*She goes off through the little door down* R.)

(*Very loud booing and cat-calls.*)

JOE (*coming off the inner stage*). Hear that ? There's somebody at the back there 'ud get such a pug in the lug——

(*Makes for pass-door* R., *but is stopped by* MRS. JOE.)

MRS. JOE. Now, Joe ; now, Joe. It's bad and I don't doubt it's deliberate, but don't let's have vulgarities.

(*She walks bravely on to the inner stage and is greeted in the now familiar fashion. She tries to sing her song—" Just a Song at Twilight "— and only gets through half of it. She comes off, horribly agitated, flings herself into* JOE's *arms. During song,* JOE *makes attempts to go on the inner stage, but is held back by the others down* R.)

(*Sobbing.*) I've never been so insulted not since that awful time at Grimsby, when they threw the fish.

(*Faints in* JOE's *arms.*)

(JOE *carries her off stage down* L.)

(NUNN *hurries on the inner stage.*)

NUNN (*addressing the audience*). Ladies and gentlemen——

(*Cries of* " Shirrup ! " " Order, *please* ! " " Sh-sh-sh ! " " Gerroutcher," " Give order, *please*," " Send 'em out," " Oh, put a sock in it "—*etc.*)

On behalf of my fellow artistes, I'd like to appeal to those members of the audience at the back there to keep quiet.

(*Cries of* " Hear, hear ! " *and* " Keep quiet yourself ! ")

I'd like them to remember that other people have paid their money and want to hear the show properly.

(*Cries of " Turn 'em out ! "* JERRY *enters from down* L. *and uses resin board,* R. SUSIE *follows and also uses resin board.*)

All we want is fair play and British sportsmanship, and to be given a chance to entertain you to the best of our ability. And now, continuing our request programme, Gatford's great favourites, Miss Susie Dean and Mr. Jerry Jerningham, will sing " Slippin' Round the Corner."

(SUSIE *and* JERRY *go on and are applauded. They sing about two lines, also dancing.* JERRY *lifts her on to his shoulder, when cabbages, etc., are thrown. The noise at the back of the audience begins again, and something is thrown from the audience which hits* SUSIE. *It is a small cabbage.* SUSIE *cries and stops.* INIGO *also stops.* NUNN, *who has been in the wings, rushes on the stage, followed by* JOE *and* MITCHAM. *The following speeches are all said together.*).

NUNN. Please give order, ladies and gentlemen. I appeal for fair play. To sportsmanship. To firm British instincts !

JOE (*picking up the cabbage*). For two pins I'll come down and knock your blasted heads together.

MITCHAM. Shame ! For shame ! And you call yourselves men ? Cowards all ! Cowards !

(*A moment's silence. From the audience can be heard* MONTE MORTIMER, *crying :*)

MONTE. Disgraceful ! Why can't you people keep quiet there ? Put the house-lights on.

(*Applauding and booing.* JOE *flings the cabbage back into the audience. Several missiles are flung on to the stage.*)

MITCHAM (*shouting into the wings*). House-lights ! Quick !

(MISS TRANT *enters quickly through the pass-door* R., *followed by two or three roughs, and behind them is* MORTIMER, *who is saying, " Let me talk to them ! "*)

OAKROYD (*after switching on the house-lights*). Hey, what do you want ?

1ST ROUGH. Coming on the stage.

2ND ROUGH. Gairr away.

(*Struggle.*)

OAKROYD. Nar, tak' your hook.

MONTE. Let *me* go on and talk to them. I'll soon smooth 'em down.

MITCHAM. You can't come on the stage.

(*The* 1ST ROUGH *attacks* OAKROYD *who, defending himself, leaves the switchboard. The* 2ND ROUGH *gives* OAKROYD *a shove in the back, then goes to the switchboard, and plunges the whole place in darkness. There is a tremendous row in the auditorium, cries of " Lights up ! " and " Send for the police ! " etc. Meanwhile there are sounds of a struggle round the switchboard.)*

JOE *(coming from the inner stage, in the darkness, roaring at the top of his voice).* I'll shift some of you. You just take that.

(Sound of somebody getting a crack on the chin, then the thud of some-body falling.)

That's one of 'em. Where's the rest. Get to the lights, one of you.

OAKROYD. I've got 'em. *(Switches on.)*

*(*JOE *knocks* MORTIMER *down. The two* ROUGHS *are not visible.)*

INIGO *(coming down* R.*).* My God, Joe, you've knocked out Monte Mortimer.

(There is a scream from MRS. JOE. *Another* ROUGH *suddenly appears, while* INIGO *has stepped forward, and turns off the lights again. Events now move very quickly indeed. The place is a bedlam. People are heard running and struggling in the dark. Fire effects, noises, etc.)*

VOICE *(off stage).* Fire ! Fire !

(This is repeated all over the place : " Fire, fire, fire ! ")

OAKROYD. There's no fire. Where's t' fire ?
MITCHAM *(shouting from the inner stage).* No fire. No fire at all. Keep your seats, please.

(There are huge crashes all over the place. Further cries of " Fire, fire ! " and " Get them lights on ! " and " Police ! " " Fetch the police ! " There is a further crash followed by a sudden drift of smoke from the right near the stage ; the smoke increases. Through this smoke all the members of the Troupe and MISS TRANT *and* OAKROYD *go running to and fro. The act drop comes half-way down up stage end.)*

OAKROYD *(to* MISS TRANT, NUNN, JOE, MRS. JOE*).* Look out ! Get out o' t' way, sharp !

(A ROUGH *crosses up stage, knocks down pylon* L. *Other* ROUGHS *join in general fight.* JOE *switches lights on.* MISS TRANT *is lying* O. *with her head by pylon.* OAKROYD *lifts her head on to his knee. Others gather round for picture. There are sounds of police whistles and the noise of a fire-engine.)*

(See Plan 12.)

CURTAIN.

Scene 12

Scene.—*Corner of a dressing-room in the Gatford Hippodrome.*

Time.—*An hour later.*

(*See Photograph of Scene. Very small set.*)

Susie *is discovered, seated* c. *dressed in her street clothes. She is white and tired, and is bending listlessly over the table. There is a pierrot hat and green costume on a basket* l. *There is a knock at the door.* Inigo *enters* R. *He is still in his pierrot costume, and very grimy.*

Inigo (R.C.). I got through to the hospital. It's not so bad, after all.

Susie (C., *recovering her natural eagerness*). Tell me about Miss Trant. Quick! (*Leans over back of chair.*)

Inigo (*sits on* R. *corner of dressing-table*). They say she's only suffering from shock and a bad arm. She'll be all right soon.

Susie. Thank the Lord for that! And what about Jimmy?

Inigo. He's got a crack on the head and they're keeping him there to-night, but he'll be out to-morrow. There won't be any song and dance for him for a week or two, though.

Susie (*growing listless again*). I'm glad it's no worse.

Inigo (R.C., *rising*). I should think so. It's good news. (*Looking at her.*) Cheer up, Susie. It'll be all right. (*Producing case.*) Have a cigarette?

(Susie *shakes her head and gives a little wave of the hand. Then she tries to smile at him. There is another knock at the door.*)

Oakroyd (R., *opening door but not appearing*). Is there onnybody at home?

Susie. Come in, Jess.

(Oakroyd *comes in smoking his pipe. He is very grimy and obviously tired, but still cheerful.* Inigo *sits again on table.*)

Oakroyd (R., *just inside door*). We're t' last here, I think, except yon sergeant up there. He wor more bother nor he wor worth, yond sergeant. He wor waar ner a pike sheep head, as we say i' Yorkshire. But I've been talking to t' Inspector. He towd me what they said at t' hospital. It's better ner like, isn't it?

Inigo. It is. And what did the Inspector say to you?

Oakroyd. Nay, it's what I said to Inspector. I towd him it 'ud ha' been all nowt if they hadn't gone an' shouted " Fire " like that. An' I towd him who started it all—them chaps at back. They've got one on 'em, but they can't get nowt out on him.

Inigo. They won't.

Oakroyd. Happen not. But I towd him it wor a proper put-up job and that them chaps had come to make bother.

Susie. Of course they did. Pigs!

INIGO. That's obvious. But we can't prove it.

OAKROYD. Not yet we can't. But I've got summat at back o' my mind that 'ud surprise some fowk. An' I'll tell yer what I'm going to do.

INIGO. What are you going to do, Jess lad?

OAKROYD. I'm going to put my thinking-cap on. Two an' two 'ull mak' fower i' this place, just as well as they will up our way, d'you see?

INIGO. No, I don't see.

OAKROYD (*turning away* R.). Never mind. I'll say no more. But aaa—by gow!—who'd ha' thowt when we started to-night——

SUSIE. Don't begin. Just keep quiet, Jess lad. It's been a mess, an awful mess. It started so wonderfully, and now it's all gone.

INIGO. You're done in, Susie. (*Comes round* L. *of* SUSIE *and kneels.*) Come on—we ought to be going home.

SUSIE (*wildly*). Going home. I was going to sing that, wasn't I?

(*She sings some of the song in a wistful broken fashion. She breaks off finally in a sudden outburst of sobbing and* INIGO *takes her in his arms and raises her to her feet.*)

INIGO (L.C., *consoling her*). Don't, Susie, don't. It doesn't matter, darling, everything'll be all right.

SUSIE (C., *she has her head on his shoulder*). It's all gone. (*Sobbing it out brokenly.*) Miss Trant's hurt—and she'll lose all her money—the show's broken up—and Monte Mortimer's gone—I've lost my chance—you've lost yours, too——

INIGO. It doesn't matter a bit. You'll soon have another just as good.

OAKROYD (R.C., *awkwardly patting her shoulder*). Nay, lass. Nay, lass. Don't tak' on like that.

SUSIE (*laughing and crying. Turns to* JESS, R.C.). Nay, lad. Nay, lad. I can't help it. But I'll stop. (*Turns to* INIGO, L.C.) Oh, I am a fool. (*Drying her eyes.*)

INIGO. You're not.

SUSIE. I am.

INIGO. You're not. You're marvellous. And I adore you.

SUSIE. Darling! (*Kisses him.*)

OAKROYD. Oh, well, if you're going to do a bit o' courtin', I'm going home by me-sen. I hadn't thowt about it, but I'm right peckish nar. It's late. But happen there'll be a bit o' meat-and-tater pie warmed up. Yon landlady o' mine is great on meat-and-tater pie. (*Makes for door* R.)

SUSIE (*goes to* OAKROYD). We're coming, too. And I hope there's a pie a yard deep waiting for you, Jess lad. (*She slips one arm in* INIGO'S *and the other in* OAKROYD'S.) And I don't want to talk about to-night any more.

OAKROYD. Well, lass, we're not dead yet, though I seem to be stiff'ning a bit.

INIGO. That's the stuff.

OAKROYD. Aye, we're not dead yet, and summat'll turn up. Put your best foot fo'most and off we go.

(*They go out, arm-in-arm and in step*, R.)

BLACK OUT.

SCENE 13

SCENE.—MISS TRANT'S *sitting-room at the " Crown," Gatford. A door to hall* L.C. *At back a large bow window looking out on a picturesque view of the town. The room is very sunny and pleasant.* (*See Photograph of Scene. Medium set.*)

MISS TRANT *is sitting on a sofa* R.C. *At table* GOOCH *is seated*, C. *He is an elderly, pleasant lawyer. He has papers and a despatch-case. It is obvious that they have been talking at some length.*

GOOCH. No, no, there's no doubt you're responsible for the damage. It's there in the contract. You'd no separate insurance, had you ?

MISS TRANT. No, I hadn't.

GOOCH. Well, you can't get away from the contract. It's a bad contract, but you signed it, and therefore you made yourself responsible. That's clear, isn't it ?

MISS TRANT. It seems to me horribly clear. According to you, we're simply helpless, and that's that.

GOOCH. Ah, but wait a minute. I didn't say that. You're responsible to the theatre people, but who's responsible to you ? In short, who really did the damage ?

MISS TRANT. I don't see that helps me much. A gang of unknown roughs—— (*Shrugs.*)

(*There is a knock on the door.*)

Come in !

(SUSIE *and* INIGO *enter* L.)

SUSIE. Good afternoon, Miss Trant.

INIGO. Good afternoon.

MISS TRANT. How nice of you two to come. Just the people I wished to see.

GOOCH (*rising, to* MISS TRANT). Look here, I don't want to bother you with all this just now, but I think you'd better know the line I'm taking. May I come back in about half an hour or so ?

MISS TRANT. Do.

GOOCH. Very well. Then I'll leave my papers here till then.

(*He goes off by the door L.*)

SUSIE. Is there any news ? (*Cross to c. below table.*)

MISS TRANT (*wearily*). All I can gather is that I'm responsible for all the damage that was done last Saturday.

SUSIE (C.). Oh, what a shame !

INIGO (L.). It's too disgraceful.

MISS TRANT (R.C.). If there is anything else, I don't understand what it is. I wish solicitors wouldn't be so grand and mysterious. You can't get them to talk like human beings. Have you heard anything from that London man ?

SUSIE (L.C.). What ? From Monte Mortimer ? I should think we have. Read it to her, Inigo.

INIGO (L., *producing letter*). It's from his secretary. (*Reads.*) " Dear Sir, I have communicated your yesterday's wire to Mr. Mortimer, who is still unable to visit the office, and he requests me in reply, to tell you and all your troupe to go to the devil. Yours truly, J. Hamilton Levy." And that's that.

SUSIE (L.C.). Yes, the mean beast. I'm glad Joe's punch knocked him silly.

MISS TRANT. I'm so sorry.

SUSIE. Oh, it's not as bad for us as things are for *you*, Miss Trant. I wish I could do something.

INIGO. Yes. We can pull through somehow. But we can't allow you to be ruined over this. We simply can't.

MISS TRANT. It seems to be a bad business for all of us. Poor Good Companions. What about the others ?

INIGO. I somehow think Mr. and Mrs. Joe'll fix up with Bourne-mouth. But of course——

(*A knock on the door.*)

MISS TRANT. Now, who can that be ? Come in !

(*Enter* LADY PARTLIT, *magnificent and important. She leaves the door open.*)

LADY PARTLIT (*coming up to* MISS TRANT, R.C., *who rises*). I hope you won't think it frightfully tiresome of me. You've been so wonderfully sweet to the entire company. I simply *had* to come and see you.

MISS TRANT (R., *bewildered, shaking hands*). It's very kind of you, I'm sure.

LADY PARTLIT. I'm Lady Partlit, you know. At least I was until this morning. (C., *calls out.*) Jerry ! Jerry !

(*Enter* JERRY L., *resplendent. He is carrying a bowl of hyacinths.*)

JERRY (*crossing to* MISS TRANT *and bowing*). From urs bath.

MISS TRANT (*taking it*). Thank you so very much, Jerry. (*She sets the bowl on a table.*)

(JERRY *goes* L.)

SUSIE (*realizing the truth, and pointing dramatically*). You've got married !

(INIGO *hums three bars of the " Wedding March."*)

LADY PARTLIT ⎱Yes—this morning.
JERRY.   ⎰

MISS TRANT ⎱(*shaking hands with* LADY PARTLIT). Oh—congra-
INIGO.   ⎰ tulations !

SUSIE (L.C., *going over to* JERRY L.). Marvellous, Jerry. (*Shaking hands.*) Let's see—will you be Lord Partlit now ?

JERRY (L.). Rorther nort. Jerst plain Jerry Jerningham, mai dear—though nort tew plain, ai hope. In farct, Jerry Jerningham up there. (*Waves his hand.*)

SUSIE. Up where ? What do you mean ?

JERRY. Electric lights, mai dear Susie. Charftesbury Avenue. J. C. Memsworth presents Jerry Jerningham.

SUSIE. *Not Memsworth, Jerry.* I don't believe you. (*Turns to* LADY PARTLIT.) Lady Partlit—I mean Lady Jerningham—I mean Mrs. Jerningham—Jerry's telling me the most awful lies——

JERRY (*languidly, to* LADY PARTLIT). You tell them, dawling.

LADY PARTLIT (C., *beaming*). But of course, darling. That's what I came to do, and we haven't much time either. You see, I own most of the shares in Mr. Memsworth's company——

MISS TRANT (R.C.). Mr. Memsworth——?

SUSIE (L.C.). Yes, he's a tremendous West End Manager.

LADY PARTLIT. And I made him come down last week to see Jerry—and of course the rest of you too, my dear. And he wants Jerry to star in his new musical comedy. And he wants to see you both as well.

SUSIE. Inigo and me ?

INIGO (*above* SUSIE). Susie and me ?

SUSIE. He wants to see us ? But where is he ?

LADY PARTLIT. He's here in Gatford, my dear, and going back to London to-night.

SUSIE. Here ! And wants to see us ? Do you hear that, Inigo ? Let's see him quick, before somebody hits *him* on the nose, too.

JERRY. Thart's whai we were looking for you—everywheah.

SUSIE. Angels. For us ? Come on, Inigo. Come on, everybody.

(*She grabs* INIGO *and pushes him towards the door. They stay above the door* L.)

JERRY. Good afternoon, Miss Trant. Good afternoon. We must run, darling.

LADY PARTLIT. Run? Certainly. Run anywhere, darling.

(JERRY *and* LADY PARTLIT *exit* L.)

SUSIE (*to* MISS TRANT). But you're coming, too—aren't you, Miss Trant?

MISS TRANT. No, my dear. Not I. I'm afraid the theatre is over for me.

SUSIE (*returning to her and sitting on* L. *end of sofa*). Oh, I'm so sorry. Don't think me a selfish pig.

(INIGO *crosses behind table and stands at back of sofa,* C.)

MISS TRANT. Don't be silly. It's a huge load off my mind. I believe it's going to be splendid for you, my dear.

INIGO. Well, anyhow, whatever happens—we can't thank you enough for what you've done for us, Miss Trant.

SUSIE. No, indeed we can't.

MISS TRANT. You've done just as much for me—if not more. You've let me see life—a thing I'd never had the chance of doing before. And no matter what the upshot of all this is going to be— nothing can ever take that away from me. Good-bye, my dear. (*She embraces her.*)

SUSIE. Good-bye, Miss Trant!

(*She hurries off to hide her feelings,* L.)

INIGO. We meet again? (*Comes down* C.)

MISS TRANT (R.C.). But of course. Soon. Perhaps at your wedding.

INIGO. I'm afraid that's as far off as ever. Susie won't listen to me. She always laughs and tells me not to be silly.

MISS TRANT. She's too young to marry yet. Life's too amazing. But one fine day, when she's had all the fun that success can bring an actress, she'll suddenly be ready to march off to the nearest registry office.

INIGO. So long as it isn't with another man.

MISS TRANT. It's for *you* to see that it's not. Stick to her. You'll never find a nicer girl. If you don't mind taking the advice of someone who's missed her own chance of happiness.

INIGO. I wouldn't say that, Miss Trant. We never know what's in store for us, do we? Good-bye!

MISS TRANT. Good luck!

(INIGO *hurries off* L.)

(MISS TRANT *looks after him, picks up the bowl of bulbs, buries her face in it, and goes and places it in the sun in the bow window.* GOOCH *and* OAKROYD *come in* L.)

OAKROYD (L.C., *wistfully*). I'm right glad to see you up again, Miss Trant. You're looking champion.

(GOOCH *sits behind table* C.)

MISS TRANT. Thank you. *(Sits on sofa R.C.)* You've come here with Mr. Gooch ?

OAKROYD. That's right. With him. *(Points at GOOCH.)* He said I'd better tell yer me-sen.

MISS TRANT. But what's all this about ?

OAKROYD (L. *of table*). Well—after that there do o' Saturday, I puts my thinking-cap on.

GOOCH (C.). That's the way. Thinking-cap !

OAKROYD. And I suddenly remembers what a friend o' mine 'ad said to me more 'n a week ago : " There's bother comin' to t' Good Companions," he says. " You mark my words."—I didn't tak' much notice o' time. But after, when I begins to puzzle it out I thowt : " 'Ow did 'e know we was going to 'ave bother ? " That's what I thowt.

GOOCH (*wagging his head to* MISS TRANT). That's the way. Thinking-cap again.

MISS TRANT. Go on, Mr. Oakroyd. This is exciting.

OAKROYD. So I sets off to look for him, for 'e'd left Gatford, you see. And I comes on one chap 'at 'ad seen him and he puts me on to another chap. Aaaa, it wor a business. But at finish up, I found him.

MISS TRANT. Was he far from here ?

OAKROYD. Forty or fifty mile away, and just setting off to go another forty or fifty. He's allus on t' move. But I got 'im at last and brought him to Mr.—er——

GOOCH. Gooch !

OAKROYD. Aye, that's it, Mr. Gooch !

GOOCH. We'll have him in now.

*(*OAKROYD *goes to the door and calls out.*)*

OAKROYD. That's right. Come on, lad.

*(*JOBY JACKSON *enters.*)*

This is 'im, Miss Trant—Joby Jackson.

JOBY. 'Afternoon, miss.

OAKROYD (*passing* JOBY *in front of him to table* L.C.). Nar, Joby lad, yer can tell 'em yer-sen.

*(*OAKROYD *sits below door* L.)*

JOBY (L. *of desk* C.). Well, Miss, it's like this—see ? I'm here in Gatford, and I'm in a boozer one morning, the " Black Bull." Know it ?

GOOCH. Corner of Castle Street. Little old place.

JOBY. That's it. Well, I'm in there, see—having one with some o' the lads. Well, in comes a feller—a biggish bloke, all dressed up, smartish feller. One or two o' the lads knows him, see ?—done a bit o' work for him some time. Nods here and there, friendly like,

calls the landlord and orders drinks all round. Sensation in Court.
Then when the landlord's gone and we're all well stuck into the
pig's ear——

Miss Trant. What ?

Gooch (*turning to* Miss Trant). He means when they were
drinking their beer.

Joby. All right, that's what I said, isn't it. (*Turns to* Oakroyd.)
Well, this feller sort o' gathers us round, and he says quiet like,
" Any o' you men like to earn some easy money ? " And he goes
on gassin' and gassin'. And some'ow—I dunno—I didn't care for
the looks o' the feller. There was too much winkin' and lookin'-
over-the-shoulder-like abaht him. So I turns me back on 'im. But
I could 'ear 'im talkin' to the other blokes—gettin' at 'em—in a
smooth roundabaht sort o' voice. " Why don't yer ? " he kep'
sayin'. " It's only a little joke on my part. That's all it is. Come
on ! A quid each of you for sittin' at the back o' the Hip and givin'
the show the bird, and another ten bob if it pans out all right."

Miss Trant. So those were the men then. But why ? I don't
understand. Who was this man ?

Gooch. Now we come to it. Who was he ?

Joby (*slowly*). I heard his name, 'cos, as I say, some of 'em knew
him——

Gooch. Good ! What was it ?

Joby. That's it. I've forgotten it. Clean gone. And me with
a memory—my God !—that's won me more pints o' beer in bets
than you (*points with hat at* Gooch) could swallow from now to
Christmas.

Gooch. But can't you remember anything about him ? What
did he look like ?

Joby. Look like ? Let's see. Biggish bloke. Clean-shaved.
Reddish face. Baggy under the eyes, poached-egg style. Too much
whisky.

Gooch. Half the men I know here look like that.

Joby. Had a funny way of suckin' up his breath through 'is
teeth every now and then—like he was drinking soup. (*He imitates*
Ridvers.)

Miss Trant. Wait a moment. He did that, did he ? After
each sentence ?

Joby. Well, I don't know 'ow many sentences 'e's 'ad.

(*Turns to* Oakroyd, *and* Oakroyd *laughs*.)

Miss Trant. I wonder if by any chance it's the man who tried
to bully me the other day downstairs, and was awfully rude and
disagreeable—a beast of a man, in fact. He has something to do
with cinemas !

Joby. Pitchers ! That's right. He spoke o' pitchers. You
know—filams.

Gooch. His name wasn't Ridvers, was it ?

JOBY. You've got it! 'It it in one!

(*Shakes* GOOCH'S *hand violently.*)

You get the coconut. Ridvers, that's it!

(*Turns and shakes hands with* OAKROYD, *who rises.*)

GOOCH (*grimly*). Ridvers! (*Rises and packs papers in wallet.*) I know Ridvers and Ridvers knows me. Leave him to me, Miss Trant. He's had his little joke, and this is where he pays for it. (*To* JOBY.) Come to my office at ten to-morrow. (*To* MISS TRANT.) Don't you worry, Miss Trant. We'll be able to settle this now, and to our satisfaction. Good afternoon. Good afternoon.

(*Crosses and goes off with his papers,* L.)

MISS TRANT. Well done, Mr. Oakroyd. Whatever happens I'm very, very grateful to you. You've been wonderful finding all this out for us.

OAKROYD (*crosses* JOBY *to* R. *of him*). Nay, *I've* done nowt, miss. It's Joby here who'll ha' done t' trick.

MISS TRANT. No, it's really you. But tell me what are you going to do now that we're broken up?

OAKROYD. Nay, I've been so throng wi' this business, I don't fairly knaw. I'll ha' to think about it.

MISS TRANT. See me here to-morrow morning, will you?

OAKROYD. Aye, I will, miss. Nar, Joby lad, yer mun come an' ha' a bit o' tea wi' me. I towd t' landlady yer would.

(*There is a knock on the door.*)

Shall I answer it, miss?

MISS TRANT. Please do.

(OAKROYD *crosses and opens the door* L.)

LANDLORD (*at the door*). Mr. J. Oakroyd. That's you, isn't it? A boy just brought this. It came to your lodgings.

(*Hands over telegram and exits, closing door.*)

OAKROYD (*coming down* L.C., *reading slowly*). "Come at once mother bad Leonard." By gow! It's from our Leonard. He'd nivver ha' sent this if his mother hadn't been right bad. I knew there were summat. I did. I knew.

MISS TRANT (*rising*). I'm so sorry, Mr. Oakroyd. You'd better get off at once.

JOBY (L. *of* OAKROYD). Come on, George, I'll set yer going. The old trouble-and-strife, eh? Bad, eh? That's ruddy hard lines, George. Aw, that's rotten. Hope for the best, though, hope for the best. Come on, George. There's a train to Bruddersford in about an hour. I'll see you on it. (*Goes to door, opens it and stands by it.*)

OAKROYD (*with a little sad shake of his head*). On t' road again, eh ? Aye, I'll be off. (*Looks at* MISS TRANT, *nods and gives her a miserable little smile.*)

MISS TRANT (C., *holding out her hand*). You shall hear from me. I have your address.

OAKROYD. Right you are—Miss Trant.

(*They shake hands. Then he goes out with* JOBY. MISS TRANT *looks after him.*)

BLACK OUT.

SCENE 14

SCENE.—*A subway in Gatford Railway Station. Steps on* L. *The rest is a long tiled passage with a sign* R. "*Platform 4. London and South.*"
    (*See Photograph of Scene. Front cloth.*)

Noises of trains above and quick incidental music throughout. The various members of "The Good Companions" *appear on the* R. *and cross and go up by the steps* L. *to the London platform.*

    First a RAILWAY PORTER *crosses with bags, then* MR. JOE *and* MRS. JOE,—*when* C. *she finds her shoelace is untied.* JOE *comes back and ties it for her. They exit* L.

    MITCHAM *next with his banjo, then* NUNN *carrying birdcage with black cat inside. Next* PORTER *with truck. Next* JERRY *and* LADY PARTLIT (*running*). *Next* INIGO *and* SUSIE. INIGO *stops* C., *draws* SUSIE'S *attention to hoarding, kisses her, she slaps his face, then kisses him and they hurry off* L.

BLACK OUT.

SCENE 15

SCENE.—*Living-room in Oakroyd's house, Bruddersford. Same as Act I, Scene 1.*

TIME.—*Late in the afternoon.*

The scene is identical, except that the room is cleared of all its furniture except an old box, C. *His basket is on another box under the window. His cap is on the basket.*
    (*See Photograph of Scene.*)

OAKROYD, *dressed in black, is sitting on* C. *box smoking his pipe, obviously thinking not very cheerful thoughts. He stays like that for about a minute or so.* OAKROYD *rises and sends blind up. Then* LEONARD, *also in a dark suit with a black band round his arm, and looking a quieter and more decent lad, than the* LEONARD *we saw in Act I, Scene 1, enters from up* R.

LEONARD (C., *quietly*). What are you going to do ?

OAKROYD (L.C.). Wait a bit, lad, wait a bit, I'll see. We can't all be barbers wi' jobs i' Manchester round t' corner, can we ?.

LEONARD. I was only asking.

OAKROYD. That's all right, lad. (*Pats him on shoulder.*) Tak' no notice. I'm glad you can look after yer-sen. (*Looking at him with something like approval.*) I fancy yer mother knew yer a lot better nor I did, and you were a good lad to her. I towd her so in t' infirmary and . . . aaa !—I never told her owt in all her life —poor soul—'aa pleased 'er better. (*Halts as if to shake off an unpleasant memory. Turns* L.)

LEONARD (L.C.). Why don't you go to our Lily in Canada ?

OAKROYD (L.). 'Cos, for one thing, I haven't brass to go wi', and for another thing, I haven't been asked—and I don't go where I'm not wanted. (*Goes down to fireplace* L.)

(*A pause during which* LEONARD *gets his hat from box under window.*)

(*Turns to* LEONARD.) Aaaa, I haven't got my tools back from Sam Oglethorpe. Must have them.

LEONARD. Gor, you made me jump, Pa. Is that all ?

OAKROYD. Aye, lad. 'It's enough an' all. I want summat to work wi' when I start. I'm a tradesman, you see, lad—and if you ask me, there's noan so damn' monny on us left.

LEONARD (C.). Can you wonder—wages they pay ?

OAKROYD (L.). Happen not. For all that, a chap 'at's learnt his trade and can use his hands—he isn't a machine and he isn't a flippin' monkey—he's a man, lad, wages or no wages, a *man* ! (*Bangs his fist on the mantel.*)

(*It is answered by a bang on the door. Two letters are thrown in ;* LEONARD *picks them up.*)

LEONARD (C.). One for me and one for you. (*Hands it over.*)

OAKROYD (L.C.). Happen Miss Trant's written me a line again. Nay, it's not. (*Opens letter and cheque falls out. Picks this up, looks at letter, then at cheque, then from one to the other.*) Here, I've gotten a hundred pounds. Aaaa, it's out of all reason. A hundred pound. That's right, isn't it ? (*Holds it out to* LEONARD.)

LEONARD. Well, I'll be blowed. What you got that for, Par ? Let's have a look. (*Takes letter.*)

OAKROYD (L.). Read t' letter out, lad—you've had more schooling nor me.

LEONARD (L.C., *reading rather laboriously*). " Dear Sir, Following the instructions of our client, Miss E. Trant, upon the satisfactory termination of our negotiations with Mr. Ridvers, we have pleasure in handing you herewith our cheque, on behalf of Miss Trant, for £100 (One hundred pounds), receipt of which kindly acknowledge to us. Goring, Son, and Gooch.''

OAKROYD. Gooch, aye, Mr. Gooch.—I knaw him. He's t' lawyer chap 'at were doing this job.

LEONARD. You must have saved her a right lot o' money. Wish I had it. (O., *examines cheque.*) I know a bit about these things. You'll have to pay it into t' bank.

OAKROYD (L.O.). What bank? I've got no bank!

LEONARD. You goes to the bank with this, and you pays it in, and then, if you want it—money, y' know—you take it out again.

OAKROYD. Pay it in and tak' it out. I call that daft. Still, if that's t' way, I'll do it. Aaaa, but a hundred pounds!

(*There is a knock at the outer door* R.O., *and it is opened by* SAM OGLE-THORPE, *carrying* OAKROYD'S *bag of tools.*)

OGLETHORPE. Na, Jess. (*Comes in.*)

OAKROYD. Na, Sam. (*Rushes to him.*)

OGLETHORPE. I've just come down to bring you your tools.

OAKROYD (*takes tool-bag from* OGLETHORPE *and puts it on box under window*). Sam, I've just gotten a hundred pounds.

LEONARD. Come in handy, that little lot. Well, see you later, Par. (*To* OGLETHORPE.) Good-bye.

(*Goes off into street,* R.O.)

OGLETHORPE. Good-bye—a hundred pounds. Nar ar's that come abaht, like? (R.O.) Wor it that business ye told me abaht t'other day—yer knaw—at t' funeral tea? That theayter woman yer got aht o' t' mess, like?

OAKROYD (O.). That's it. (*Crosses to* L.)

OGLETHORPE. Well, that'll gi yer a bit of a start, like, if there's owt yer fancy. But listen, Jess lad. (*He sits on box* O. *and lights his pipe.*)

OAKROYD. Aye, I'm listening, Sam. (*Comes and sits on box* O., *to* L. *of* OGLETHORPE.)

OGLETHORPE (*very earnestly*). Whativver tha does, Jess, keep aht o' t' joinery and jobbing i' this neighbourhood, that's all. Way things is nar, it's nowt—nowt at all, it isn't. It's just like t' hens scrattin' for a bit o' summat.

OAKROYD. Is it waar ner it wor?

OGLETHORPE. Nay, trade's so bad they'll ha' owt done, d'yer see, Jess? Folk hasn't a bit o' brass to spare. Might be different dahn south, I daresay, but here—it's nowt. Keep to the theayter line, I say.

F*

OAKROYD. Nay, it's all up wi' theayter job nar, Sam. " Good Companions " is brokken up.

OGLETHORPE. Tired o' your travels ?

OAKROYD (*wearily*). Well, I don't knaw.

OGLETHORPE. Here, Jess. Did yer ivver get to Bristol and Bedfordsheer ?

OAKROYD (*puzzled*). Bristol and Bedfordsheer ?

OGLETHORPE. Don't tell me yer nivver got there, Jess.

OAKROYD (*slowly, rather sadly*). I remember. Well, I nivver got to Bristol, Sam, though I've nivver given it a thowt, I may ha' seen Bedfordsheer, but I don't knaw fairly. I've been all ower t' shop—up and down and across—on t' road, yer knaw. Aye, I've seen a deal.

OGLETHORPE. Then yer owt -to be satisfied, nar, lad.

OAKROYD. Are we *ivver* satisfied, Sam ? (*Pauses. Slowly, wistfully.*) Places is more alike than yer'd think when yer comes to have a good look at 'em. And it isn't places as counts—it's fowk. (*Puts his hand on* OGLETHORPE'S *knee.*)

OGLETHORPE. For a chap as has just gotten a hundred pound, you're a bit down in t' mouth. Don't quite know what to do wi' thi-sen, like, eh ?'

OAKROYD. Aye, summat o' t' sort.

OGLETHORPE (*after regarding him sympathetically for a moment, rises, with a brisk change of tone*). Well, I mun be off. Happen I'll see thee later, Jess. (*Makes for door* R.C.)

OAKROYD. Aye, so long, Sam.

OGLETHORPE. Behave thy-sen, Jess.

(*He goes to door. After a second,* OGLETHORPE *is heard at the door.*)

(*Outside the door.*) Don't be so daft. Give it to me. Well, what of it ? I've known him thirty year, lad, and you've never set eyes on him. Here, Jess—(*comes down* R.) there's a sort o' telegraph lad asking for you.

(OAKROYD *rises and takes cable from* SAM OGLETHORPE, R.)

OAKROYD (R.C., *reading the cable*). Aaaa, by gow ! It's from our Lily. Listen, Sam. She says "*Very grieved. All love. If you come out here very welcome and good job any time. Lily, Jack.*" Do you hear, Sam ? *If you come out here very welcome and good job any time.* Sam, she wants me to go, she wants me to go. (*Crosses to* L.)

OGLETHORPE (R.C.). Aye, seems as if she does. But yer won't go to Canada, will yer ?

OAKROYD. By gow, I will. (*Goes up to box below window.*)

OGLETHORPE. Aaaa, but it's a long way off.

OAKROYD (*puts cap on, picks up tools and basket*). Long way ! Long way, nowt ! If it wor from here to t' moon, I'd go. (*Rushes to the door.*) Hey up, lad !

The stage is immediately darkened as OAKROYD *speaks his last words, the scene is cleared, then a spot light is fixed on* OAKROYD, *who is seen walking away from the audience, with his little trunk in one hand and his bag of tools in the other.   As he walks, he is seen mounting in the gangway of a liner, and the liner can be heard hooting above the sound of the orchestra.*

   (*See Photograph of Scene.*)

CURTAIN.

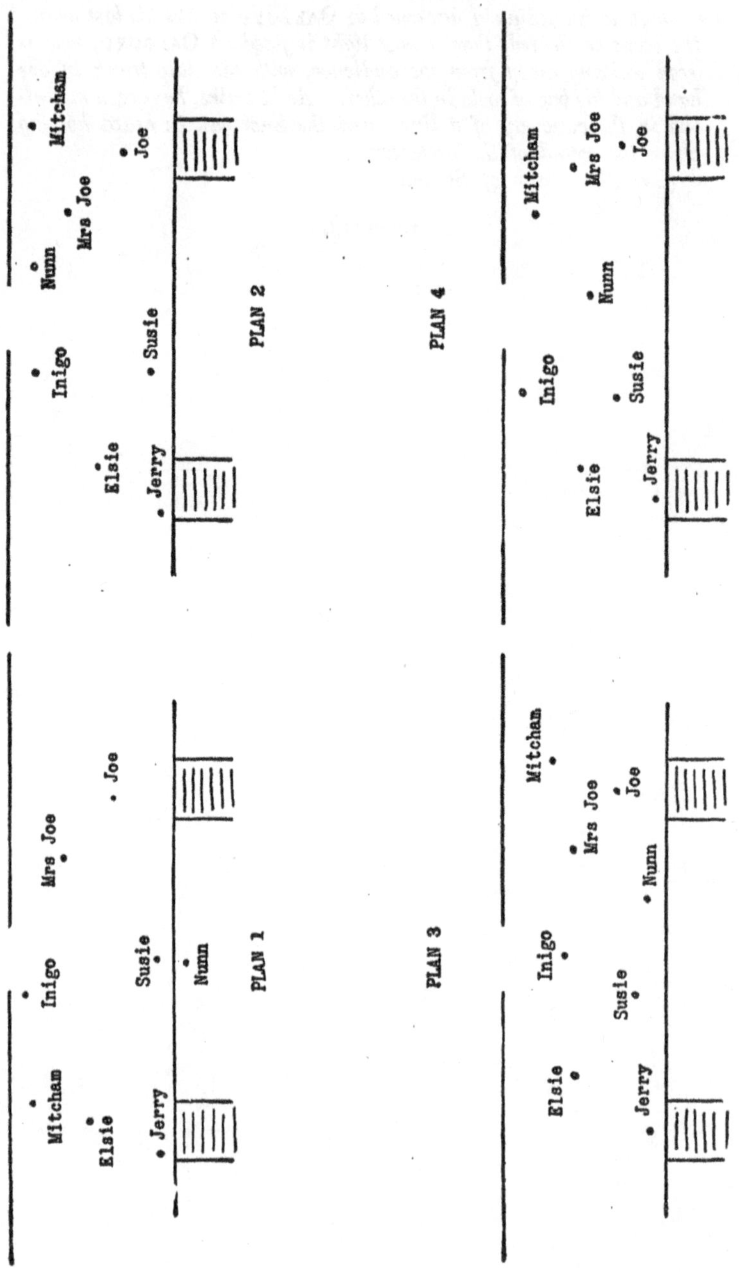

Mitcham

Elsie

Inigo

Susie

Mrs Joe

Jerry

Nunn

Joe

PLAN 1

Mitcham

Nunn

Mrs Joe

Inigo

Susie

Joe

Elsie

Jerry

PLAN 2

Mitcham

Elsie

Inigo

Susie

Mrs Joe

Jerry

Nunn

Joe

PLAN 3

Mitcham

Inigo

Mrs Joe

Elsie

Nunn

Joe

Susie

Jerry

PLAN 4

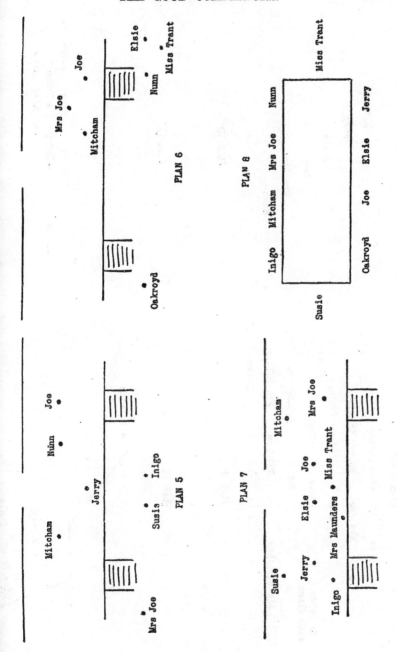

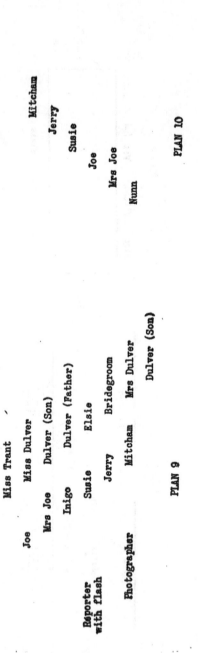

PROPERTY PLOT

This Property Plot is intended as an addition to the information given at the commencement of each scene, which, in most cases, tallies with the photographs.

ACT I

SCENE 1

Essentials are :
  Kettle at fireplace.
  Poker at fireplace.
  Shirt on clothes-horse.
  Tea-things on table.
  Iron and ironing-board on table.
  Iron at fireplace.
  Kipper on plate at fireplace.
  OGLETHORPE'S hat on sewing-machine.

Off Stage.
  Pasty on plate off R. for MRS. OAKROYD.
  Dilapidated suitcase and box off L. for ALBERT.
  Bag of tools off L. for OAKROYD.
  Insurance card and money off L. for OAKROYD.
  Pipe, tobacco and matches off L. for OAKROYD.
  Gramophone and records off L. for ALBERT.
  Small basket trunk off R. for OAKROYD.

SCENE 2

Essential is :
  Folding map on motor-car seat.

Off Stage.
  Tumbler and glass-cloth for EFFIE.
  Small theatrical basket for EFFIE.
  Pound note for EFFIE.

SCENE 3

Essentials are :
  Soda syphon and bottle of whisky on desk L.
  Tumbler of whisky and soda on piano.
  Tumbler of whisky and soda for FAUNTLEY, who is seated C. on a small Chair
  Music on piano.

Off Stage.
  Banjo off L. for MITCHAM.
  Trick bunch of flowers off L. for TARVIN.
  Knapsack off L. for INIGO.

Noise Effect.
  Clock strike, nine, off L.

89

Scene 4

Essentials are :
Packet of " Woodbine " for JACKSON.
In motor-van : 2 rubber dolls, biscuit tin, filled teapot, army mess-tin, cup, condensed milk in open tin with spoon.

Off Stage.
Bag of tools and basket trunk off R. for OAKROYD.
Filled pipe and matches off R. for OAKROYD.

Noise Effect.
Pistol shots off L.

Scene 5

Essentials are :
Linoleum L.
Rubber dolls and animals on stall O.
Bell for BELLMAN.

Off Stage.
Envelope and small package off R. for ENVELOPE MAN.
Whistle off R. for POLICEMAN.

Scene 6

Essentials are :
Leather coat on seat of car.
Gloves on seat of car.
OAKROYD'S basket trunk and bag of tools on ground R.
EFFIE's theatrical basket in back of car.

Off Stage.
Nil.

Scene 7

Essentials are :
Note-book for NUNN.
Pound note in hand-bag for ELSIE.
Knitting for MRS. JOE.
Copy of " The Stage " on end chair L.

Off Stage.
Banjo off R. for MITCHAM.
EFFIE's theatrical basket off L. for OAKROYD.
Shopping-bag with vegetables off R. for MRS. MAUNDERS.
Ten-shilling note in hand-bag off L. for MISS TRANT.

Scene 8

Essentials are :
Glasses with port.
Big spoon for NUNN to conduct with.
Banjo for MITCHAM.

Off Stage.
Nil.

ACT II

Scene 9

Essentials are :
Flashlight in working order for REPORTER.
Cigarette-case in pocket for JERRY.
Folded poster in pocket for NUNN.
Flapjack in hand-bag for SUSIE.
Telegraph form in drawer of writing-table.
Pencil in writing-table pen-tray.

Off Stage.
2 soup plates with dry rice off R. for NUNN.
Small tumbler with whisky and soda off R. for LANDLORD.
Cigar off R. for RIDVERS.

SCENE 10

Essentials are :
Music for ETHEL.
INIGO's hat and coat on piano.
Off Stage.
Nil.

SCENE 11

Essentials are :
Short stools on stage.
Resin board down R.
Off Stage.
Cabbages and various missiles to throw from R.
Noise Effects.
Boos and catcalls off R.
Applause off R.
Police whistles off R.
Fire-engine bells off R.

SCENE 12

Off Stage.
Cigarette-case with cigarettes off R. for INIGO.

SCENE 13

Essentials are :
Papers and despatch-case for GOOCH.
Off Stage.
Letter off L. for INIGO.
Bowl of hyacinths off L. for JERRY.
Telegram off L. for LANDLORD.

SCENE 14

Off Stage.
Bags off R. for PORTER.
Banjo off R. for MITCHAM.
Birdcage with black cat inside off R. for NUNN.

SCENE 15

Essentials are :
LEONARD's hat on box under window.
OAKROYD's basket trunk on box under window.
OAKROYD's cap on basket trunk.
Off Stage.
Two letters, one with cheque inside, off R. to go through letter-box.
OAKROYD's bag of tools off L. for OGLETHORPE.
Cable off R. for OGLETHORPE.

SCENE 1

SCENE 2

SCENE 3

SCENE 4

SCENE 5

SCENE 6

[*Photographs by the Stage Photo Co.*

SCENE 7

SCENE 8

[Photographs by the Stage Photo Co.

SCENE 9

SCENE 10

SCENE 11

SCENE 12

[*Photographs by the Stage Photo Co.*

SCENE 13

SCENE 14

[*Photographs by the Stage Photo Co.*

SCENE 15

SCENE 16

[*Photographs by the Stage Photo Co.*

Printed in May 2023
by Rotomail Italia S.p.A., Vignate (MI) - Italy